# BUS REVIEW
## 13
### Review of 1997
#### Published 1998

C000225686

Yorkshire Coastliner, the first operator of the Alexander Royale body, came back for more in 1997. It took four on Volvo Olympian chassis, bringing to ten the number in the fleet. They had 72 coach seats. *Alexander*

Front cover: The new Arriva livery started to appear on new vehicles towards the end of the year. The first Arriva-liveried buses to come from Alexander's factory were two ALX200s on Dennis Dart SLF chassis for Derby City Transport. They were allocated to a park-and-ride service. *Alexander*

Back cover, upper: Unusual new buses for FirstBus were UVG-bodied Dennis Dart SLFs. These were bought from stock to enable Kelvin to launch services in the Irvine and Kilmarnock area in competition with Stagecoach. *Billy Nicol*

Back cover, lower: The take-over of Tayside Transport by National Express saw major changes in Dundee. The company started trading as Travel Dundee and was allocated 20 new Volvo B10Ls with Wright bodies, diverted from Travel West Midlands. The red, white and blue Travel West Midlands livery will be applied to other single-deckers in the Travel Dundee fleet. *Billy Nicol*

# Contents

Plaxton's Verde, launched in 1991, came to an end in 1997 with a batch of dual-door bodies on Volvo B1OB chassis for City of Oxford. The Verde never achieved the popularity of its smaller stablemate, the Pointer, an example of which is just visible behind. *SJB*

First published 1998

ISBN 0–946265–27–5

© Bus Enthusiast Publishing Company, 1998

Typeset in Times and Helvetica

Electronic page makeup by Jeremy Scott

Published by

Bus Enthusiast Publishing Company

5 Hallcroft Close, Ratho, Newbridge

Midlothian EH28 8SD

Bus Enthusiast is an imprint of

Arthur Southern Ltd.

# Introduction

CORPORATE LIVERIES. Enthusiasts love to hate them. At the start of 1997 there was but one nationwide corporate colour scheme - the ubiquitous Stagecoach white-with-stripes. At the end of the year there were three. Stagecoach was followed by FirstGroup - rather half-heartedly it would seem - and then by Arriva, as the Cowie Group had become.

The off-white base adopted by FirstGroup has prompted comparisons with Stagecoach amongst bus users, while the stylish new interior which goes with it quickly saw the new vehicles being dubbed Barbie Buses (or should that be BarbieBuses?) - referring to the doll of the same name.

Arriva's turquoise and biscuit is arguably the boldest and most stylish of Britain's corporate bus colours - but for enthusiasts, if not for customers, any attraction the new liveries hold will quickly pall when it is realised that wherever you go in Britain you're unlikely to be far from a bus the same colour as the ones in the last town you visited.

Buses are an important part of the urban street scene. Bright liveries like those used by North Western, Bristol City Line, Northumbria and PMT - to pick a few at random - do much to enliven the towns and cities they serve. Dull and unimaginative liveries - Greater Glasgow's red being the worst culprit? - have the reverse effect.

Apart from these major new liveries - launched too late in the year to have any real impact, although they will spread rapidly in 1998 - the other major developments of 1997 revolved around take-overs and new models. Stagecoach, Cowie, Go-Ahead and FirstGroup all expanded to a greater or a lesser extent.

The significant new models were Britain's first low-floor double-deckers (discounting much earlier candidates for the title, such as the Bristol Lodekka). At Coach & Bus 97 there were low-floor 'deckers from DAF, Dennis (for Hong Kong) and Volvo with bodies by, respectively, Optare, Alexander and Northern Counties. The last-named - known as the Plaxton President - was the star of the show although while Plaxton were justifiably proud of their new product Volvo were peculiarly reticent. That the President will go from strength-to-strength is certain - but quite where Volvo's unusual chassis is going is far from clear. None of the new low-floor models had entered service by the end of the year.

Orders announced around the time of Coach & Bus 97 included two which raised a few eyebrows, both from Stagecoach. First was an order for 100 Dennis Tridents for operation in London - the only Dennis 'deckers supplied new to Stagecoach have been Dragons for Malawi. Then came an order for 150 MAN single-deckers - easily MAN's biggest-ever UK bus deal and business which most observers would have expected to go to Volvo, Stagecoach's established supplier of full-size single-deckers.

It's no secret that Stagecoach drives a hard bargain with its suppliers. It will be interesting to see who wins the next big Stagecoach order.

A side effect of the Stagecoach orders will be a reduction in Volvo's share of the UK bus market. Volvo leads in coach sales, with Dennis in the number two spot. But in bus sales Dennis are - just - the leaders, thanks to the ubiquitous and ever-popular Dart. Volvo will no doubt remain number two, but with a reduced market share, as DAF (supplying Arriva), Scania (winning business from FirstGroup), Dennis and now MAN win sales at the Swedish manufacturer's expense.

The next few years will be interesting ones indeed, with variety in vehicle types compensating for standardisation in liveries.

The arrival of new types means the withdrawal of older ones. Travel West Midlands' last Fleetlines were withdrawn in 1997. Greater Glasgow's last Atlanteans will vanish in 1998. Old-generation types with big operators - Fleetlines, Atlanteans, VRTs, Leopards, Nationals - are fast disappearing.

To keep up with developments in the industry, *Buses* provides regular up-to-date information, while the PSV Circle's news sheets provide a wealth of data for those interested in the detail of who's buying what.

*Stewart J Brown*
*Reedley Hallows, 1998*

In 1996 FirstBus ordered 207 Mercedes-Benz minibuses with Plaxton bodies. Deliveries started in the summer of 1997 and included eight for Eastern National, as seen here in Chelmsford. With the Vario Mercedes-Benz has consolidated its position as the leading supplier of minibuses to UK operators. *SJB*

# FirstBus goes corporate - well, sort of

THE YEAR got off to an indifferent start for FirstBus, with the announcement in January that it had to sell Midland Bluebird (including the SMT operations in Edinburgh) and one of its Glasgow area depots. This followed an inquiry by the Monopolies & Mergers Commission into the group's acquisition of SB Holdings in May 1996, a take-over which made FirstBus the dominant operator in an area which swept from Dumbarton, to the west of Glasgow, right across central Scotland to Edinburgh and south to the English border. The sale was to be completed by the end of 1997. It wasn't.

The group's Glasgow woes continued in February when concerns over maintenance saw the Scottish traffic commissioner cut the fleet authorisation on the operating licence of its GCT subsidiary from 150 to 120 vehicles. But, on top of the MMC and the traffic commissioner, there was even worse to come in Glasgow. In April Stagecoach launched new services in

Scotland's biggest city, starting with a fleet of 20 Volvo B6LE and five B10Ms. These ran to housing estates on the southern and eastern edges of the city - competing head-to-head with FirstBus subsidiary Strathclyde Buses.

FirstBus was quick to respond. It snapped up some stock Volvo B10Ms with Plaxton bodies - as well as a couple of Irizar-bodied Scanias - and launched new express services between Glasgow and Cumbernauld to compete with established Stagecoach routes. Kelvin introduced services in Ayrshire, using Dennis Dart SLFs with UVG bodies - also purchased from manufacturer's stock. And in June Lowland started running in Fife, using the all-over red Strathclyde Buses livery and trading as FifeFirst. The FifeFirst services were centred on Dunfermline and used 17 low-floor Scanias and three Dennis Dart SLFs. The Dennises were new, as were some of the Scanias; others were transferred to Fife from elsewhere in FirstBus. The re-appearance of red buses in Fife

brought back memories of Scottish Bus Group days; Alexander (Fife) used a red livery in the days before Stagecoach.

In Glasgow FirstBus branded some vehicles as SuperBus - but the effect was less than convincing. The vehicles were Alexander PS-types in Strathclyde Buses' drab unrelieved red and looked anything but Super.

FirstBus was not strongly represented in London at the start of the year. Its only presence was through Thamesway on tendered services in the north and east. That changed in March, with the purchase of CentreWest, the former London Buses subsidiary which served west and north-west

*FifeFirst was the FirstBus response to Stagecoach's attack on its Glasgow operations. Controlled by Lowland Omnibuses, it was launched with low-floor Dennises and Scanias painted in Greater Glasgow's red livery. The Dennises were Darts with Plaxton bodies. SJB*

London, and also had a base in Orpington. CentreWest brought with it the Bee Line operation in Berkshire and Buckinghamshire, and London Buslines.

A smaller takeover in March was that of Streamline of Bath by Bristol Omnibus. The Streamline name and colours were retained.

There was further expansion in the south in July, with the purchase of Southampton Citybus, the former municipal operation which had been privatised in a management-led employee buy-out in 1993. The company ran 140 buses, including Dennis Darts powered by compressed natural gas.

Coincidentally, CNG was in the news at Northampton Transport, with the arrival in the fleet of six Volvo B10Ls powered by CNG. FirstBus also runs a CNG-powered bus - a Dart - in Bristol, and had a further CNG-powered Dart on order for Bristol for delivery in 1998. Another trial of alternative power got underway in Portsmouth in February when

Provincial put a hybrid bus into operation. This was a second-hand seven-year-old Mercedes 609D with Reeve Burgess body - which might be indicative of a certain lack of serious commitment.

Transport enthusiasts had breathed a collective sigh of relief at the start of 1996 when FirstBus had unveiled its corporate identity which left existing liveries untouched but adopted a new corporate-style fleetname. At the end of 1997 that started to change. In November FirstBus was renamed FirstGroup - and it announced a corporate livery of off-white relieved by sweeping blue and magenta stripes at skirt level.

The first of the FirstBus high-specification Pointer 2s were delivered in company liveries and included vehicles for Bristol City Line, Greater Glasgow, Provincial and, as seen here, Greater Manchester in a new cream-based livery. Deliveries at the end of the year were in the new corporate colours. *SJB*

But, and it's a big but, the new livery was only to be applied to low-floor buses or to new deliveries built to a new FirstBus body specification which had been announced in the summer. This featured bright colour co-ordinated interiors, more generous seat spacing and double-glazing where it could be fitted (which excluded

PMT was one of the first companies in the FirstBus group to put Mercedes-Benz Varios in service. It took 27 with Plaxton Beaver 2 bodies. *SJB*

Bus wars in Glasgow saw a range of non-standard types join the FirstBus fleets in Scotland. These included eight East Lancs-bodied Dennis Darts for GCT. *SJB*

minis or double-deckers because of the added weight). New heating and lighting systems were included, with the whole aim being to raise the image of public transport.

Now it doesn't take too long to work out that this livery policy means that it will be a very long time - like 15 years - before the last of the old colour schemes disappears if it is only being applied to modern buses, which carries the risk of creating the impression of a two-tier service. Methinks there will be a rethink before long. Can you imagine Boots adopting a new corporate identity but only applying it to new shops? Of course you can't.

With the new livery comes the fleetname First, the f-logo, plus, on the side of the vehicle, the operating company's trading name. The first First buses were Wright-bodied Scanias.

Before the new livery was announced Greater Manchester started to abandon its traditional orange, taking delivery of new low-floor buses in what was the old GRT advance livery. This used an off-white base with squiggles of colour on the side - Midland Bluebird's blue was Greater Manchester's choice. It started to appear on new Plaxton-bodied Dennis Darts and Wright-bodied Scanias in the autumn. Darts delivered earlier in the year were orange. Clearly these accessible buses will ultimately be candidates

for repainting in corporate FirstGroup colours.

New vehicle orders were announced in November for a total of 786 buses. They marked something of a change of direction from the 1996 order in which Plaxton-bodied Darts had dominated. Orders for Darts were down from 257 in the 1996 announcement to 100 in the 1997 programme.

Wright of Ballymena did particularly well, winning orders for 350 bodies on Scania and Volvo chassis. The Volvos included 40 articulated buses - easily the biggest artic order ever placed in Britain. The double-deckers were once again Volvo Olympians and the minibuses were again Mercedes Varios with Plaxton Beaver 2 bodies. Orders

for just over 100 buses for CentreWest were to be confirmed.

Deliveries in 1997 included large numbers of Dennis Dart SLFs with Plaxton Pointer bodies - including the first of the re-styled Pointer 2s. More unusual Dennises were Lances with Northern Counties bodies for Eastern National. It seems fair to forecast that they will be the last Lances. There were also Wright-bodied Scanias for a number of fleets. Double-deckers were Volvo Olympians with Alexander Royale bodies - notably in Glasgow and Leeds - and in smaller numbers with Northern Counties Palatine II bodies for operation in Glasgow and Bristol.

## FIRSTBUS ORDERS 1998-1999

| Double-deck | |
|---|---|
| 100 | Volvo Olympian/Alexander |
| 25 | Volvo Olympian/Northern Counties |
| 30 | low-floor to be decided (for CentreWest) |
| **Single-deck** | |
| 170 | Scania/Wright |
| 140 | Volvo/Wright |
| 55 | Dennis Dart SLF/Plaxton |
| 45 | Dennis Dart SLF/TBA |
| 40 | Volvo/Wright articulated |
| 76 | midis to be decided (for CentreWest) |
| **Minibuses** | |
| 105 | Mercedes Vario/Plaxton Beaver |

Northern Counties supplied bodies on long-wheelbase Olympians to FirstGroup, with Greater Glasgow getting ten Palatine IIs. Similar buses were delivered to Bristol. *SJB*

## FIRSTGROUP

Aberdeen Bus (not trading)
Brewers
Bristol Omnibus Co
    Badgerline
    City Line
    Durbin
    Streamline
Broch Cymru (Badger Wales)
(not trading)
Berks Bucks Bus Company
    Bee Line
CentreWest London Buses
    Challenger
    Ealing Buses
    Heathrow Fast
    London Buslines
    Orpington Buses
    Uxbridge Buses
Eastern Counties
    Blue Bus
    Rosemary Coaches
Essex Bus
    Eastern National
    Thamesway
Grampian Transport
    Beaver Bus
Greater Manchester Buses North
Kirkpatrick of Deeside

Leicester Citybus
Lowland Omnibuses
    Ian Glass
    SMT
Mainline Group (20 per cent)
Mairs of Aberdeen
Midland Bluebird
    SMT
Midland Red West
    Citibus
Northampton Transport
Oban & District*
PMT
    Crosville
    Pennine
    Red Rider
Provincial
Rider Group
    Bradford Traveller
    Calderline
    Kingfisher
    Leeds City Link
    Quickstep Travel
    Rider York
South Wales Transport
Southampton Citybus
    Hants & Sussex

Strathclyde Buses
    GCT
    Greater Glasgow
    KCB Network
    Kelvin
    SB Travel
    SuperBus
Wessex Coaches
    Sky Blue
Western National
    Roberts


Great Eastern Railways
Great Western Trains*


* minority shareholding

At the start of the year FirstBus was receiving the last of its old-style two-step single-deckers with the delivery of 13 Dennis Lances to Eastern National. These had Northern Counties Paladin bodies. Production of the Lance effectively came to an end in 1997 as operators switched to the low-floor Dart SLF. *SJB*

Among the first restyled Plaxton Pointer 2s was a batch of 16 for Provincial. Early deliveries were in cream and red, but later buses arrived in the new corporate FirstGroup scheme. The Pointer 2 has new front and rear mouldings. *SJB*

A small number of full-size Mercedes were delivered to FirstBus - a throwback to the vehicle policy which had been pursued by GRT Holdings. They had Optare Prisma bodies. A Lowland Omnibuses example leaves Galashiels bus station. *SJB*

Long-wheelbase Volvo Olympians with Alexander Royale bodies appeared in two FirstBus fleets in 1997 - Greater Glasgow and Leeds City Link. Leeds got 16. They had just 72 seats, despite being 10.3m long, as part of a drive by FirstBus to improve passenger comfort. FirstBus has 144 Royales on order for 1997-98 delivery. *Alexander*

# 1997 round-up

**A summary of some of the key events in the bus and coach industry in 1997.**

## January

• Mercedes-Benz announces that it is to import the low-floor O405N. The basic structure will be built at Mannheim and then shipped to Britain to be completed by UVG at Waterlooville. The first order, for 100, comes from Travel West Midlands.

• Skills of Nottingham takes over Barton Buses' coaching operations.

• East Yorkshire Travel buys Armstrong-Galley from Stagecoach Busways (16 coaches).

• Q Drive buys Scancoaches of London (43 vehicles).

• Applebys of Louth take over the operations of Enterprise & Silver Dawn of Lincoln (11 vehicles).

• MTL Trust Holdings wins the Merseyrail Electrics franchise.

## February

• South Lancashire Transport withdraws its local services in Chester, started in 1995 and operated by 16 second-hand minibuses. Some of the services are taken over by PMT.

• Proctors of Bedale buys Peter Hall Coaches of Robin Hoods Bay (eight vehicles).

• Hedingham Omnibuses buys Osbornes of Tollesbury (21 vehicles). The deal takes the Hedingham fleet to 132.

• Coach Line of Rotherham is set to buy Red Ensign, the Southampton Citybus coaching operation, with six coaches. However the sale falls through (as does a bid by Coach Line for Kingstonian Coaches, owned by Thamesdown Transport). Coach Line itself goes out of business before the year ends. It had been formed as an independent company in April 1996, taking over the coaching business of South Yorkshire Transport.

• Silver Choice of East Kilbride (11 coaches) goes into receivership. It is later rescued by a management buy-out.

• Q Drive buys Eurobus, which operates scheduled services to Europe.

• The 500th low-floor Dennis Dart SLF enters service. It is for Maidstone & District.

• Buddens Coaches of Romsey buy Robin Hood Vehicle Industries. Robin Hood produce the RH2000 midicoach body.

• National Express takes over Tayside Transport. The operation is rebranded Travel Dundee.

• Minibus builders Crystals buy the rights to produce the TBP Freeway II low-floor minibus. The Freeway was to have been built by Pathfinder of Newark, who acquired the rights to the design when TBP closed in June 1996. The Freeway uses Peugeot Boxer running units.

## March

• FirstBus buys CentreWest.

• Wallace Arnold Coaches is for sale. Shearings, bought by its management from the Rank Organisation in December 1996, is widely reported to be the most likely buyer.

• Stagecoach sells its Milton Keynes operations and its United Counties Huntingdon services to MK Metro, owned by Julian Peddle. This follows an MMC ruling in 1996. The Huntingdon operations are rebranded as Premier Buses.

• Optare unveils prototype ColomboRider, based on a Chinese chassis built by Chaoyang Diesel. It is to be built in Sri Lanka, where Optare is part of a joint venture to manufacture ColomboRiders with a target production of 700 a year using CKD kits shipped from Britain.

• National Express wins the franchises for ScotRail, Central Trains and North London Railways.

• Shearings is named as the likely buyer for Wallace Arnold Coaches, drawing a strong protest from WA's workforce.

• Bova announces two new Futura variants. The high-floor FHD12.330L is powered by the DAF 8.65-litre engine previously only offered in the low-floor FLD series. A high-floor Cummins C-series model is also offered.

• West Midlands Travel buys Merry Hill Minibuses, launched in 1988 to serve the Merry Hill shopping centre in Dudley. WMT had had a stake in the company at its inception. Merry Hill Minibuses runs 40 vehicles.

• MTL absorbs Fareway, which it had purchased in 1993.

• A new owner takes over the Omni minibus, Fleetstar Tyres Ltd. The company is renamed FTL Omni. It had, as Omni Coach, been controlled by the receivers.

• London Coaches takes over the London sightseeing operations of Blue Triangle, along with nine open-top Fleetlines.

• Streamline of Bath is taken over by Bristol Omnibus. The Streamline name is to be retained.

• The first Volvo B10BLE enters service. It has a Northern Counties body and is one of five for Stagecoach Manchester.

• WG launches the S320 coach, a restyled version of the 1995 UniStar which in turn had been developed from the previous Vanguard model. It is available only on the Dennis Javelin and sells for just £105,000.

## April

• Marcopolo bodywork, built in Portugal and available on the Dennis Javelin, is in addition to be offered on the MAN 18.310 chassis. Sales are handled by Alf Moseley of Loughborough, which expects to sell 30 in 12 months.

• Buscraft of Birkenhead closes. The company had launched its 35-seat Impala body on the Mercedes-Benz 814L chassis in 1995.

• Marshall unveils new Capital body for Dennis Dart SLF. It has a strong family resemblance to Marshall's integral Midi.

• Metrobus of Orpington takes a 30 per cent stake in Leisurelink of Newhaven. Leisurelink runs 20 vehicles.

• The 3,000th Volvo Olympian to be built at the company's Irvine plant is delivered to Hong Kong Citybus. Volvo transferred Olympian production from Workington to Irvine in 1993.

• Greater Manchester PTE wins outline planning permission for a £10million guided busway from Leigh to Manchester.

• Travel West Midlands launches its fleet of 14 CNG-powered Volvo B10Ls. The 69-passenger buses, with Alexander Ultra bodies, are operating between Walsall and Wolverhampton.

• Scania launch the Irizar InterCentury on the new L94 underframe. The InterCentury is a low (3.2m-high) version of the Irizar Century range.

• Falcon Travel of Smethwick ceases operations.

• Adkins of Daventry (26 vehicles) ceases operations.

• HMB Buses launches operations in Newcastle using 22 second-hand minibuses.

• Pete's Travel of Birmingham buys Buzzways (seven buses). It takes Pete's fleet to almost 100 vehicles, mostly minibuses.

• Stagecoach launch new services in Glasgow, competing head on with FirstBus. FirstBus respond with services in Ayrshire, Fife and Cumbernauld.

## May

• Lothian Region Transport teams up with Dews of Somersham to run open-top tours in Cambridge, competing with Guide Friday.

• Wright launch low-floor Renown on Volvo B10BLE. The body has a gently ramped floor with a single shallow step ahead of the rear axle - a layout being marketed by Wright under the Floline name. The first order is for 102 for FirstBus.

• National Express Group takes a 63 per cent stake in Concordia Bus, with the balance being held by a Norwegian company. Concordia will be used to pursue privatisation opportunities in Europe.

• Stagecoach buys the 30-bus AA Buses operation from Dodds of Troon.

• Metrobus of Orpington buys East Surrey of South Godstone (23 vehicles).

• The Go-Ahead Group buys Brighton Transport. The operation is absorbed by Brighton & Hove.

• Speedlink wins the new Heathrow Hoppa hotel bus contract, requiring 26 low-floor buses to run hotel shuttle services.

• The MMC launches an inquiry into the acquisition by National Express of the franchises to run ScotRail and Central Trains.

• London Traveller is set up by former Metroline employees.

## June

• Metroline is floated on the stock exchange.

• The entire 12-vehicle fleet of Miller of Airdrie is destroyed in a fire.

• Production of the Buscraft Impala midicoach body is taken over by Crest Conversions of Doncaster.

HMB Buses was a new name on the streets of Newcastle. Its fleet included MCW Metroriders acquired from Stanwell Buses and running in their previous owner's colours. A Stagecoach Olympian in Magic Bus livery loads in the background. *SJB*

11

• Rapid Transit International unveils plans for a £35million guided busway network for Northampton, to be operated by low-floor gas buses. If it goes ahead, the aim is to complete the scheme within 10 years and to reduce car use in the town by 25 per cent by 2010. RTI is also looking at a similar scheme for Nottingham.

• Scania announces the availability of a 9m Irizar MidiCentury 35-seater for the UK - built on a MAN 11.220 chassis.

When it was first introduced the Dennis Dart was very much a London bus. Its appeal is now almost universal, but it was fitting that a London operator, Metroline, should take delivery of the 1,000th example of the low-floor SLF variant which was added to the Dart range in 1995. It is posed outside the Hindu temple in Neasden. *SJB*

• Alexander launch ALX100 minibus on Mercedes Vario chassis. It replaces the AM Sprint and has square-cornered gasket glazing. The first are delivered to Cowie subsidiaries Midland Red and Stevensons.

• A £50million guided trolleybus system is proposed for Merseyside by a consortium, Transform, which includes Cowie subsidiary North Western as one of its members. A high-frequency service from Albert Dock to Page Moss is planned, and the vehicles will incorporate "drive-by-wire" technology in which guidance is provided by cables buried under the road surface. Planned start date is 2001.

• Stuart's of Manchester cease operations.

• A new midicoach chassis is unveiled by an Ulster company - the Cannon Softline 8.500. The chassis code indicates an 8 tonne gross vehicle weight and the use of a Cummins B-series engine producing 500Nm of torque. The 135bhp Cummins engine, mounted at the front, drives the rear axle by way of a ZF five-speed gearbox. The Cannon Softline 8.500 is intended to compete with the Mercedes Vario. The chassis is exhibited at the Three Counties show in Malvern and the company plans to have a bodied vehicle ready by October. It doesn't - but the first chassis is delivered to Robin Hood towards the end of the year, for an RH2000-style body.

## July

• Concerns over maintenance see Black Prince of Leeds having its O-licence curtailed from 52 to 26 vehicles.

• McGill's of Barrhead, the last survivor of the old west of Scotland independents, is bought by Clydeside Buses.

• Months of speculation about a take-over of Wallace Arnold by Shearings come to an end when WA's management mounts a successful buy-out bid.

• Bova delivers its 5,000th integral coach. It goes to OAD, a Dutch operator.

• FirstBus buys Southampton Citybus.

• Work starts on extending Manchester Metrolink to Salford Quays and Eccles.

• Stagecoach takes over Transit Holdings' remaining UK businesses - Thames Transit (180 vehicles) and Docklands Transit (48). It also takes control of Transit Australia (120 buses).

• The 1,000th low-floor Dennis Dart enters service - with Metroline Travel.

• Leisurelink of Newhaven ceases trading. Metrobus takes over part of the operation.

• London United is bought by French company Transdev.

**Universal Buses started operating in Greater Manchester in September. Its initial fleet included Dennis Dart SLFs with UVG bodies. *SJB***

• MK Metro buys the 15-vehicle Challenger operation in Milton Keynes.

• Cornish coach company Ford's of Gunnislake ceases trading.

## August

• A new Greenways system of bus priority routes starts in Edinburgh - featuring green-surfaced bus lanes.

• NCP merges its Heathrow-based coach operations - Capital Coaches and Whyte's Airport Services - in a new Capital Logistics company.

• Catch-A-Bus, which operated 33 buses in the South Shields area, withdraws its services. The operation was started in 1986 by Hylton Castle Coaches, which continues as a coach operator.

• Consultants DCA Design produce concept drawings for a new style of low-floor double-decker for London Transport.

• The Go-Ahead Group adopts a new red and blue livery for its six subsidiaries in the north-east of England, each of which will adopt the "Go" prefix to its fleetname.

• Bland's of Cottesmore cease trading - after almost 70 years. Road Car takes over most of the company's routes.

• Optare announces that it will be supplying MetroRider chassis to Australia for local bodying.

• SC Coachcraft formed by SC Containers to build midicoaches in Rotherham. Its first, the Vision on Mercedes O817L chassis, is unveiled in November.

• MTL closes its London MTL Travel coach business, based on the R&I Coaches operation acquired in October 1995. The company ran 30 coaches.

• Cowie group's County Bus & Coach takes over the operations of West's of Woodford.

## September

• The bus operations of Wealden Beeline - and five Dennis Darts - are acquired by Maidstone & District.

• Flights of Birmingham buy Excelsior of Bournemouth (55 coaches).

• Toyota launch the wider Optimo IV midicoach with two-plus-two seating. The Optimo IV is based on the Toyota Coaster chassis and is 2.29m wide. The 2.12m wide Optimo III continues.

• EYMS splits its coach and bus businesses with the bulk of the

coach operation going to the new Godfrey Burley Group, set up by an EYMS director. Its main trading name is National Holidays, the new identity which had been adopted for the EYMS Group's coaching fleets in January, which included Charterplan in Manchester and Armstrong Galley in Newcastle.

• Universal Buses starts operations in the Stockport area. Its fleet includes two new Dennis Dart SLFs with UVG bodies and three Optare Excels.

## October

• Bowens of Birmingham takes over Yorks of Northampton (28 vehicles). Bowens is owned by the Moseley Group.

• Holmeswood Coaches takes over Bostocks of Congleton (32 coaches).

• Walls of Manchester withdraws from local bus operation. Its services are covered by Stagecoach Manchester. The company's 25 buses - mainly modern DAFs - are disposed of separately.

• Stagecoach takes over the operations - but not the 25 buses - of Walls of Manchester.

• Volvo is to buy Finnish coachbuilder Carrus. The deal is to be completed in January 1998. Carrus built 450 bodies in 1996.

## November

• FirstBus becomes FirstGroup, and announces a new corporate livery - white with blue and magenta relief.

• The Cowie group adopts a new name: Arriva. A new corporate livery follows in December for buses outside London.

• Stort Valley of Bishops Stortford takes over the operations of Travellers of Hounslow.

• The last Fleetlines operated by Travel West Midlands are withdrawn. TWM and its direct predecessors - the West Midlands PTE and Birmingham City Transport - had been operating Fleetlines since 1962.

• Flights buy Central Coachways from Travel West Midlands (17 coaches).

• FTL Omni announces a restyled model, to be launched in January. It will feature an Iveco engine.

• Machins Coaches of Ashby de la Zouch closes. Founded in 1937, it ran 16 vehicles.

• Daisy Bus Service of Brigg closes.

• Wilts & Dorset buys Lever Coaches of Salisbury (18 vehicles).

## December

• Stagecoach buys Rhondda Buses (100 vehicles).

• Arriva buys the sightseeing operations of London Coaches (81 buses).

• Stagecoach is named as the preferred bidder for the Sheffield Supertram.

• Leeds Suburban Buses starts operating between Moortown and Leeds. It is associated with the established Black Prince business.

• UVG calls in the administrative receivers to its Waterlooville factory - formerly Wadham Stringer. Most of the workforce is made redundant and the business is put up for sale.

• National Express acquires Belgian bus company Group Bronckaers.

• Henlys Group - owners of Plaxton - announces that its Prevost subsidiary in Canada (owned jointly with Volvo) is to take over another Canadian manufacturer, Nova Bus. Nova Bus produced 1,380 buses in 1996 from factories in Montreal, New Mexico and New York state.

• Larratt Pepper of Barnsley closes. Its three coaches and its premises are sold to National Holidays. The company was founded in 1907.

• National Express is ordered to sell Scottish Citylink within six months, following an MMC inquiry into its take-over of ScotRail.

Travellers, the well-known West London coach business, was taken over by Stort Valley Coaches in November. Deliveries to Travellers during 1997 included 14 Dennis Javelins with Plaxton Premier bodies. This one, operating on behalf of a Japanese tour company, is seen at Windsor. *SJB*

# More colour in the capital

THE EXPANSION of Harris Bus. The demise of Londonlinks. CentreWest being sold to FirstBus. A guarantee that Routemasters will still be running in 2002. The disappearance of Docklands Transit. The changes in ownership of major London operators which have characterised recent years actually slowed down in 1997 but, as can be seen, the year was far from dull.

Two small operators disappeared in the early part of the year. In January Blue & White Buses gave up its route from Ruislip to Northolt - a route which in one form or another had been operated by an independent for some three decades (remember Elm Coaches, or Scorpio?). The route was taken over by London Sovereign.

The other small operator to cease running a regular service in the capital was D&J International, which operated Dennis Darts between Liverpool Street Station and London City Airport. This contract was taken over by East London, with a fleet of seven Dennis Dart SLFs with Alexander ALX200 bodies in a blue livery.

FirstBus expanded into London in a big way in March, by buying CentreWest. Hitherto its only presence had been through Thamesway. CentreWest runs some 500 vehicles, which were soon acquiring corporate-style f-logos and fleetnames. While the bulk of the CentreWest operation is in west London, it also has a substantial presence in Orpington, where it trades as Orpington Buses.

CentreWest, incidentally, was Marshall's best customer in 1997, taking 41 Dennis Dart SLFs with Marshall Capital bodies (with another 26 due in 1998), and 16 of Marshall's rare integral Minibus, a type which hasn't quite taken the market by storm. It will be interesting to see if the Marshall connection survives CentreWest's change of ownership.

The two remaining buy-outs of London Buses companies underwent change in 1997.

Metroline was floated on the stock exchange in June, while London United was bought by a French company, Transdev, in July.

Harris of Grays was the operator which expanded most noticeably in 1997. In April it took over route 108, which runs through the Blackwall Tunnel and was branded as the Lewisham Link, using Optare Excels. This had previously been operated by Kentish Bus. Harris's expansion continued in the autumn with three routes in the Ilford area, taken over from East London. These were run by new double-deckers: Volvo Olympians with East Lancs Pyoneer bodies. Further expansion was due to take place in early 1998 with routes south of the Thames being taken over from Selkent and Kentish Bus.

Capital Citybus moved into central London in February with the 91, running from Trafalgar Square to Crouch End, formerly operated by MTL London Northern. For this it bought 16 Alexander-bodied Volvo Olympians in a new red and yellow livery, designed to meet London Transport's requirements that buses on new tenders in the central area be in a livery with at least 80 per cent red. The result was attractive.

In the summer Capital Citybus added nine Dennis Arrows with East Lancs Pyoneer bodies to its fleet - in standard yellow livery - for service 369 in Ilford, won from East London. Further expansion was on the cards for 1998 which resulted in orders being placed for 13 Dennis Dart SLFs and 27 more Arrows - all with bodywork by East Lancs.

Armchair expanded in Ealing in the summer, taking over the E2 from CentreWest in May. For this it bought 25 new Dennis Dart SLFs with Plaxton Pointer bodies. At the same time CentreWest bought Marshall-bodied Dart SLFs for Ealing area services which it had retained. At the end of the year Armchair was taking delivery of six Volvo Olympians with Northern Counties' handsome

Palatine II bodywork.

Staffing problems at London General saw it transfer two routes and 11 Optare MetroRiders to Epsom Buses in the autumn.

Cowie was redrawing the responsibilities of its London area businesses, which affected Londonlinks, Kentish Bus, Grey-Green, South London and Leaside. Londonlinks vanished, and Kentish Bus started to lose its strong identity, most notably with the start of a repaint programme for its Routemasters - into London red. Grey-Green took over the 66 between Romford and Leytonstone from sister Cowie company County Bus & Coach in August. Cowie was renamed Arriva in November, and the new Arriva logo quickly appeared on Cowie buses in the capital.

Q Drive had been big in west London with its London Buslines operation, sold to CentreWest in 1996. It popped up again, in a smaller way, in the same year when it took over the C10 serving the Elephant & Castle, operated by its Limebourne Coaches business. Limebourne expanded further in 1997 taking over the 42 (Liverpool Street to Camberwell Green) from Kentish Bus and the 156 (Wimbledon to Clapham Common) from London General. Both were run by low-floor Dennis Darts.

While one small independent expanded, another vanished. Docklands Transit was taken over by Stagecoach in July and absorbed into its East London fleet in October.

New buses were bought by a number of former London Buses subsidiaries. Stagecoach took Plaxton-bodied Mercedes Varios and Alexander- and Northern Counties-bodied Olympians. There were also Northern Counties-bodied Olympians for London General and London Central. Olympians with East Lancs bodies were delivered to Harris Bus and to Metrobus, the latter taking them for service 64 between New Addington and Thornton Heath, won from South London.

New double-deckers in London were mainly Volvo Olympians. These included long-wheelbase models with lowheight Alexander bodywork for Stagecoach East London. *SJB*

London Central and London General both took delivery of standard-length Olympians with dual-door Northern Counties Palatine I bodies. This is a London Central bus. London General has Palatine IIs on order for 1998. *SJB*

Metroline took Dennis Dart SLFs with Plaxton Pointer bodies - the first two-door SLFs for London since the CentreWest-liveried prototype at Coach & Bus 95. The arrival of new Darts at Metroline was matched by the departure of old ones - a reminder that the Dart has now been around for the best part of 10 years. Metroline was also looking for a buyer for its fleet of Dennis Lances.

The first low-floor buses for Grey-Green were examples of the ubiquitous Dennis Dart SLF - but with Alexander ALX200 bodies rather than the Plaxton Pointer favoured by most London fleets. There were 17.

On the Routemaster front London Central announced that it was repowering 36 of the type with Scania engines - the 115bhp 9-litre DS9 - at a cost of around £300,000. South London abandoned its distinctive livery for the RMs on the 159 which from 1994 had been running with cream window surrounds and roof. During the year they were painted in a more sober and traditional layout of all-over red with a yellow relief band. In November London General retained the contract to run route 11 (Liverpool Street to Fulham Broadway) using Routemasters, guaranteeing the type's survival until 2002! Can the Routemaster clock up 50 years of London service?

In sharp contrast to the award of a five-year Routemaster tender, was the announcement in August that 100 low-floor double-deckers would be entering service in London in 1999. Two operators, Stagecoach East London and MTL London, won contracts for five routes. Stagecoach quickly announced an order for Alexander-bodied Dennis Tridents - straight off the drawing board. By the end of the year MTL had not indicated what vehicle types it would be choosing.

The indications are that further contracts requiring low-floor double-deckers are in the pipeline. This points to London taking the lead in low-floor double-deckers, just as it did with low-floor single-deckers before they became an

industry norm.

Contract changes announced at the end of 1997 for 1998 included Travel West Midlands winning the C1 from London General. This runs between Victoria and Kensington High Street and Travel West Midlands was setting up a new Travel London company to run the service. It was expected to order Optare Solos. Travel West Midlands was last seen in the capital during its brief tenure of ownership of Westlink in 1994-95.

Other 1998 changes will see Armchair lose one route to Metroline while gaining another from London United, while TGM Buses is taking over one route each from Armchair and London United. Capital Citybus will consolidate its position as London's biggest independent with routes being taken over from Leaside Buses.

**Harris Bus became a significant force in London during 1997, with further expansion coming in 1998. New vehicles included Volvo Olympians with East Lancs Pyoneer bodies in a particularly striking livery.** *David Barrow*

**Capital Citybus adopted a new livery for 16 Volvo Olympians used on a tendered service running in central London. They had 72-seat Alexander R-type bodies.** *SJB*

# Stagecoach still expanding

EXPANSION BY Stagecoach continued in 1997, albeit at a slower pace than earlier in the decade. The first significant move in 1997 involved a sell-off rather than a purchase. In March the group sold off its operations in Milton Keynes and Huntingdon, following a ruling by the Monopolies & Mergers Commission in 1996. The new owner was Julian Peddle, who has interests in a number of small operations around the country.

The Milton Keynes fleet became MK Metro - a name already in use, albeit not very strongly - while the Huntingdon operations were rebranded Premier Buses.

Also in March the group's coach operations in Hull, Kingstonian Travel, were sold to the EYMS Group. Kingstonian had been the coaching arm of Kingston-upon-Hull City Transport and operated eight vehicles. Another coach business to be sold was Viscount Central, part of the Burnley & Pendle operation. This went to Border Buses, along with some B&P bus services in Colne and Barnoldswick. At the same time Border Buses reduced its operations over the main corridor between Nelson, Burnley and Padiham. Viscount Central ran 20 vehicles.

But, as always with Stagecoach, expansion was just around the corner. Glasgow was the venue. FirstBus was the target. Stagecoach launched new services in the city, starting with 20 Volvo B6LEs and five B10M coaches. Other types appeared, including B10M buses with Northern Counties bodies, diverted to Glasgow before being delivered to Stagecoach Manchester. B10Ms with Alexander PS-type bodies were added too. The target was said to be 150 buses by the end of the year.

The new services provoked a response from FirstBus with incursions into two of the established Stagecoach operating areas - south Fife and central Ayrshire. Whatever the effects on the two groups' profits, it was a bonanza for Glasgow bus users with more services on offer and competition on fares too. It can't last, but by the end of the year there was little sign of either of the contestants backing down.

The other significant event involving Stagecoach in Ayrshire was its purchase in May of the 30-vehicle AA Buses operation from Dodds of Troon. AA was the last survivor of Ayrshire's traditional independent bus operators. As with A1 Service before it, the decision was made to retain the AA livery for some operations and at the end of the year new AA-liveried Dennis Darts with Alexander bodies were being delivered for use on services in Irvine.

The biggest single expansion by Stagecoach came in July, with the purchase of the remaining operations of Transit Holdings in the UK - Thames Transit (180 buses) and Docklands Transit (48 buses). The group also took control of the 120-vehicle Transit Australia business. This followed the takeover in January 1996 of

The shape of things to come. Dennis issued this artist's impression of a Trident when it won the Stagecoach order for 100 buses for service in London. The body will be Alexander's ALX400, to be launched in 1998. *Dennis*

Transit Holdings' Devon businesses - which had its first low-floor buses, 14 Volvo B6LEs, in service in April.

Redrawing of operational boundaries saw Docklands Transit being absorbed by East London in October while earlier in the year, in February, the Ribble operations in Lancaster and Morecambe were transferred to Cumberland, along with 76 buses. Stagecoach Lancaster was adopted as a trading name.

Walls of Manchester, one of the city's most successful post-deregulation independents, ceased operating in October with Stagecoach Manchester taking over the company's services, but not its 25 vehicles. The Magic Bus formula, which had proved successful in Manchester, was adopted by Busways in Newcastle from April, using the same over-all blue livery for 26 Atlanteans running on lower-cost services on three cross-city routes.

In December Stagecoach strengthened its position in South Wales by buying Rhondda Buses, based in Porth. Stagecoach already owned Red & White. Rhondda, with a fleet of 100 single-deck vehicles, had come into being in 1992 following the collapse of National Welsh. Rhondda also traded as Caerphilly Busways and Parfitts - the latter an operation acquired in 1995. The most numerous type in the Rhondda fleet was the Dennis Dart, of which there were 33.

Overseas, Stagecoach sold its 250-bus Swebus Norge operation to a Norwegian company, thus concentrating its Scandinavian resources in Sweden. It also pulled out of Malawi.

On the new vehicle front Volvos continued to dominate - B10Ms and Olympians in particular, but also including (in March) the first low-floor B10BLEs to enter service in Britain. There were five, with Northern Counties bodies, for Stagecoach Manchester - a company which, incidentally, had the number of vehicles on its operating licence cut from 745 to 715 in response to concerns about maintenance. Other new vehicles for the group included Mercedes-Benz Varios with Plaxton Beaver 2 bodies. Large numbers of these went to Stagecoach Manchester and, in London red, to Selkent. Further B10BLEs, but with

## STAGECOACH GROUP SUBSIDIARIES

Bluebird Buses
   Inverness Traction
   Stagecoach
Burnley & Pendle Transport
   Whizzard
Busways Travel Services
   Blue Bus Services
   Economic
   Favourite Services
   Magic Bus
   Newcastle Busways
   South Shields Busways
   Sunderland Busways
   Tyne & Wear Omnibus Co
Cambus Holdings
   Cambus
   Millers
   Premier Travel Services
   Viscount Bus & Coach Co
Circle Line
Cleveland Transit
   Hartlepool Transport
   Kingston-upon-Hull City
     Transport
   Stagecoach Cleveland
   Stagecoach Darlington
East London Bus & Coach Co
   East London Hoppa
East Midland Motor Services
   Chesterfield Transport
Eastbourne Bus Company
   (New Zealand)
Fife Scottish Omnibuses
G&G Travel
Greater Manchester Buses South
   Magic Bus
   Stagecoach Manchester
Grimsby-Cleethorpes Transport Co

Kenya Bus Services (75 per cent)
Kenya Bus Services (Mombasa)
   (51 per cent)
Magicbus Scotland
   (Holding company)
National Transport Tokens
   (99.9 per cent)
PSV Claims Bureau
Rhondda Buses
   Caerphilly Busways
   Parfitts
Ribble Motor Services
   Zippy
Sistema Metrobus de Bogota
   (25 per cent)
South East London & Kent Bus Co
   Selkent
Stagecoach Devon
   Bayline
   Devon General
Stagecoach Glasgow
Stagecoach Graphics
Stagecoach International Services
Stagecoach North West
   Cumberland Motor Services
     Coachlines
     Lakeland Experience
     Stagecoach Lancaster
Stagecoach Portugal (25 per cent)
Stagecoach Scotland
Stagecoach South
   East Kent
   Hampshire Bus
   South Coast Buses
   Stagecoach Hants & Surrey
   Sussex Coastline
     Sussex Bus

Stagecoach West
   Aberdare Bus Co
   Cheltenham & Gloucester
   Omnibus Co
     City of Gloucester
     Gloucester Citybus
     Metro
     Stroud Valleys
   Cheltenham District Traction
   Midland Red South
     David R Grasby
     Stratford Blue
     Vanguard Coaches
   Red & White Services
Swebus
Swindon & District
Thames Transit
   The Oxford Tube
   Blackbird Flyer
   Carousel
   Kidlington Cavalier
   Rose Hill Runners
Transit Australia
   Stagecoach Australia
United Counties Omnibus Co
   Coachlink
   Street Shuttle
The Valleys Bus Co
Wellington City Transport
Western Buses
   AA Buses
   A1 Service

The Island Line
Porterbrook Leasing
South West Trains

Alexander's new ALX300 body, were ordered for 1998 and the first was on show at Coach & Bus 97.

Alexander's orders for 1997 were increased in February to include 177 ALX200s, 170 R-types and 160 PS-types.

While FirstBus was upgrading its interior specifications, Stagecoach stuck with a smart but serviceable finish. Its low-floor buses occasionally carry branding - but the general interior appearance remains little changed.

Vehicles for sale caused some comment in August with a full-page advert in *Coach & Bus Week* offering modern buses for sale with illustrations of a 1985 Busways Olympian and a 1992 Cumberland B10M. Industry observers saw this as a kite-flying exercise to find out if there would be any takers for relatively good-quality used buses rather than time-expired examples. There weren't.

New vehicle orders announced for 1998 contained a few surprises, Out went Volvo as the main supplier of single-deck buses - no B10Ms, no B10BLEs in the big announcement - and in its place came MAN with an order for 150 low-floor chassis to be bodied by Alexander. That single order was greater than the total number of MANs supplied to UK operators since the company had first appeared in this market almost 20 years earlier. Dennis, too, won a significant order for 100 Trident low-floor double-deckers. These will be the first new Dennis 'deckers for Stagecoach, although the company has bought Javelins and Darts in reasonable numbers.

Volvo wasn't the only manufacturer to lose out. Plaxton, which had won orders in 1997 for double-deckers, coaches and minibuses, got nothing in the 1998 order announcement. Those Volvo

B10Ms on order will have Jonckheere bodies. The Olympians and Mercedes minibuses will be bodied by Alexander.

The year ended with yet another diversification in view - light rail. Stagecoach operates heavy rail services through its former British Rail franchises, but in December it was named as the preferred bidder to take over operation of the loss-making Sheffield Supertram, which was apparently more Tram than Super. The franchise rules reportedly include maintaining the existing grey livery - so no white-and-stripes for Sheffield's trams.

**While most new Stagecoach buses are either red (for London) or white with stripes, a few do appear in other liveries. In 1997 these included 12 Dennis Darts with Alexander ALX200 bodies which carried the green and cream livery of AA Buses, taken over by Stagecoach in May.** *Alexander*

To launch its new Glasgow operations Stagecoach used some traditional Volvo B10Bs with old-style Northern Counties Paladin bodies, diverted from Stagecoach Manchester. *SJB*

| STAGECOACH ORDERS 1998/99 | | |
|---|---|---|
| 150 | MAN 18.220LE | Alexander ALX300 |
| 100 | Dennis Trident | Alexander ALX400 |
| 100 | Dennis Dart SLF | Alexander ALX200 |
| 100 | Volvo Olympian | Alexander R |
| 40 | Mercedes Vario | Alexander ALX100 |
| 25 | Volvo B10M | Jonckheere |

The first examples of Volvo's low-floor B10BLE to enter service were five with Northern Counties Paladin bodies, built at Wigan and delivered before the body was renamed the Plaxton Prestige and production was transferred to Scarborough. They were for Stagecoach Manchester. *David Barrow*

# Who makes what?

A guide to chassis available to UK operators in 1997, or announced in 1997 with availability for 1998.

| Make and model | Engine position | Overall-length (m) | Wheel-base (m) | Engine | Cubic capacity (l) | Power (bhp) | Gearbox | Speeds |
|---|---|---|---|---|---|---|---|---|
| **BOVA integral (Holland)** | | | | | | | | |
| Futura FHD12-340 | RV | 12.0 | 6.09 | DAF WS242 | 11.6 | 329 | ZF S6-85 | 6 M |
| Futura FHD12-330L | RV | 12.0 | 6.09 | DAF RS200 | 8.65 | 333 | ZF S6-85 | 6 M |
| Futura FHC12-300 | RV | 12.0 | 6.09 | Cummins C | 8.3 | 300 | ZF S6-85 | 6 M |
| Futura Club FLC | RV | 12.0 | 6.09 | Cummins C | 8.3 | 275 | ZF S6-85 | 6 M |
| Futura Club FLD | RV | 12.0 | 6.09 | DAF RS245M | 8.65 | 388 | ZF S6-85 | 6 M |
| Futura FHD10-340 | RV | 10.0 | 4.89 | DAF WS242 | 11.6 | 329 | ZF S6-85 | 6 M |
| **DAF (Holland)** | | | | | | | | |
| DB250 | RV | 9.9 | 5.05 | DAF RS200 | 8.65 | 272 | Voith D851.3 | 3 A |
| DB250LF | RV | 10.4 | 5.45 | DAF RS200 | 8.65 | 272 | Voith D851.3 | 3 A |
| Gearbox options - ZF 5HP500, Voith D854.3 | | | | | | | | |
| SB220 | RH | 11.6 | 5.50 | DAF LT160L | 11.6 | 218 | ZF 4HP500 | 4 A |
| SB220 GS | RH | 11.9 | 5.50 | DAF GS160 | 8.65 | 218 | ZF 4HP500 | 4 A |
| SB220ULF | RH | 11.5 | 6.00 | DAF GS160 | 8.65 | 218 | ZF 4HP500 | 4 A |
| SB220GG | RH | 11.6 | 6.00 | DAF GG 170 LPG | 8.65 | 231 | ZF 4HP500 | 4 A |
| Gearbox options - ZF 5HP500, Voith D851.3, Vouth D854.3 | | | | | | | | |
| SB3000WS | RV | 11.9 | 6.02 | DAF WS242 | 11.6 | 330 | ZF 8S-140 | 8 M |
| **DENNIS (UK)** | | | | | | | | |
| Dart | RV | 8.5 | 3.78 | Cummins B | 5.9 | 130 | Allison AT545 | 4 A |
| Dart | RV | 9.0 | 4.30 | Cummins B | 5.9 | 130 | Allison AT545 | 4 A |
| Dart | RV | 9.8 | 5.12 | Cummins B | 5.9 | 130 | Allison AT545 | 4 A |
| Dart SLF | RV | 9.0 | 4.40 | Cummins B | 5.9 | 130 | Allison AT545 | 4 A |
| Dart SLF | RV | 10.0 | 5.20 | Cummins B | 5.9 | 130 | Allison AT545 | 4 A |
| Dart SLF | RV | 10.5 | 5.81 | Cummins B | 5.9 | 145 | Allison AT545 | 4 A |
| Super Pointer Dart | RV | 11.3 | 5.95 | Cummins B | 5.9 | 160 | Allison B300R | 4 A |
| Javelin | UV | 8.5 | 4.00 | Cummins C | 8.3 | 211 | ZF S6-85 | 6 M |
| Javelin | UV | 10.0 | 5.00 | Cummins C | 8.3 | 245 | ZF S6-85 | 6 M |
| Javelin | UV | 12.0 | 6.25 | Cummins C | 8.3 | 245 | ZF S6-85 | 6 M |
| Javelin GX | UV | 12.0 | 6.25 | Cummins C | 8.3 | 300 | ZF S6-85 | 6 M |
| Lance | RV | 10.5 | 5.05 | Cummins C | 8.3 | 211 | ZF 4HP500 | 4 A |
| Lance | RV | 11.0 | 5.85 | Cummins C | 8.3 | 211 | ZF 4HP500 | 4 A |
| Lance | RV | 11.5 | 5.85 | Cummins C | 8.3 | 211 | ZF 4HP500 | 4 A |
| Arrow | RV | 10.5 | 5.05 | Cummins C | 8.3 | 245 | ZF 4HP500 | 4 A |
| Trident | RV | 9.9 | 5.25 | Cummins C | 8.3 | 220 | ZF 4HP500 | 4 A |
| Trident | RV | 10.5 | 5.80 | Cummins C | 8.3 | 220 | ZF 4HP500 | 4 A |
| Trident engine option - 245bhp rating | | | | | | | | |
| **IVECO (Italy/Spain)** | | | | | | | | |
| DailyBus 49.10 | FV | 6.36 | 3.60 | Iveco 8140.27S | 2.5 | 104 | Iveco 2826 | 5 M |
| DailyBus 49.10 | FV | 6.76 | 3.95 | Iveco 8140.27S | 2.5 | 104 | Iveco 2826 | 5 M |
| DailyBus 59.12 | FV | 7.04 | 4.18 | Iveco 8140.47S | 2.5 | 116 | Iveco 2826 | 5 M |
| DailyBus 59.12 | FV | 7.64 | 4.48 | Iveco 8140.47S | 2.5 | 116 | Iveco 2826 | 5 M |
| EuroMidi | FV | 9.73 | 4.63 | Iveco 8060.45B | 5.86 | 177 | Iveco 2855.6 | 6 M |
| EuroRider 29 | RV | 12.0 | 6.15 | Iveco 8640.41R | 9.5 | 290 | ZF S6-85 | 6 M |
| EuroRider 35 | RV | 12.0 | 6.15 | Iveco 8640.41T | 9.5 | 350 | ZF 8S-180 | 8 M |
| EuroRider Interurban | RV | 12.0 | 6.15 | Iveco 8640.41R | 9.5 | 290 | ZF 5HP600 | |
| **KASSBOHRER integral (Germany)** | | | | | | | | |
| Setra S250 | RV | 12.0 | 6.08 | Mercedes OM442LA | 15.1 | 381 | ZF 8S-180 | 8 M |
| Setra S250 | RV | 12.0 | 6.08 | Mercedes OM442LA | 15.1 | 381 | Allison | 6 A |
| Setra S250 | RV | 12.0 | 6.08 | MAN D2866 | 11.9 | 370 | ZF 8S-180 | 8 M |
| **MAN (Germany)** | | | | | | | | |
| 11.220 bus | RV | 10.0 | 4.9 | MAN D0826 | 6.9 | 220 | ZF 4HP500 | 4 A |
| 11.220 coach | RV | 9.0 | - | MAN D0828 | 6.9 | 220 | ZF S6-36 | 6 M |
| 13.220 bus | RV | 10.0 | 4.7 | MAN D0826 | 6.9 | 220 | ZF 4HP500 | 4 A |
| NL222F | RH | 11.7 | - | MAN D0826 | 6.9 | 220 | Voith D851.3 | 3 A |
| 18.310 | RV | 12.0 | - | MAN D2866 | 11.9 | 310 | ZF S6-85 | 6 M |
| 18.370 | RV | 12.0 | - | MAN D2866 | 11.9 | 370 | ZF 8S-180 | 8 M |
| **MARSHALL integral (UK)** | | | | | | | | |
| Minibus | RV | 8.5 | 3.94 | Cummins B | 3.9 | 135 | Allison AT545 | 4 A |
| Minibus | RV | 8.5 | 3.94 | Perkins Phaser | 4.0 | 135 | Allison AT545 | 4 A |

## MERCEDES-BENZ (Germany)

| Model | Pos | | | Engine | | bhp | Gearbox | |
|---|---|---|---|---|---|---|---|---|
| 709D | FV | 6.94 | 4.25 | Mercedes OM364A | 3.97 | 86 | Mercedes G2 | 5 M |
| 711D | FV | 6.94 | 4.25 | Mercedes OM364A | 3.97 | 105 | Mercedes G2 | 5 M |
| 811D | FV | 7.49 | 4.80 | Mercedes OM364A | 3.97 | 105 | Mercedes G2 | 5 M |
| 814D | FV | 7.49 | 4.80 | Mercedes OM364A | 3.97 | 136 | Mercedes G3 | 6 M |
| Vario O-814D | FV | 6.94 | 4.25 | Mercedes OM904LA | 4.25 | 136 | *ZF 5S-42 | 5 M |
| Vario O-814D | FV | 7.49 | 4.80 | Mercedes OM904LA | 4.25 | 136 | *ZF 5S-42 | 5 M |
| O1120L | FV | 9.15 | 4.84 | Mercedes OM366LA | 5.96 | 211 | Mercedes G4 | 6 M |
| O404 Vita | RV | 12.0 | 6.25 | Mercedes OM441LA | 10.96 | 340 | Mercedes GO4 | 6 M |
| O405 | RH | 11.6 | 5.88 | Mercedes OM447H | 11.97 | 213 | ZF 4HP500 | 4 A |
| O405N | RH | 12.0 | 5.88 | Mercedes OM447H | 11.97 | 213 | ZF 4HP500 | 4 A |

* Allison AT542 automatic offered as an option.

## NEOPLAN integral (Germany)

| Model | Pos | | | Engine | | bhp | Gearbox | |
|---|---|---|---|---|---|---|---|---|
| N4014 | RH | 12.0 | 6.02 | MAN D2866 | 11.9 | 230 | ZF 5HP500 | 5 A |
| Jetliner N212H | RV | 9.85 | 4.75 | Mercedes OM401LA | 9.6 | 290 | ZF S6-1600 | 6 M |
| Cityliner N116 | RV | 12.0 | 5.45 | MAN D2866 | 11.9 | 400 | ZF 8S-1600 | 8 M |
| Cityliner N116 | RV | 12.0 | 5.45 | Mercedes OM441LA | 10.96 | 340 | ZF S6.1600 | 8 M |
| Skyliner N122/3 dd | RV | 12.0 | 5.55 | Mercedes OM402LA | 12.8 | 381 | ZF 8S-1600 | 8 M |
| Skyliner N122/3 dd | RV | 12.0 | 5.55 | MAN D2866 | 11.9 | 370 | ZF 8S-1600 | 8 M |

## OPTARE integral (UK)

| Model | Pos | | | Engine | | bhp | Gearbox | |
|---|---|---|---|---|---|---|---|---|
| MetroRider 4 | FV | 7.7 | 4.75 | Cummins B | 5.9 | 130 | Allison AT545 | 4 A |
| MetroRider 4 | FV | 8.5 | 4.75 | Cummins B | 5.9 | 130 | Allison AT545 | 4 A |
| Solo M850 | RV | 8.5 | 5.53 | Mercedes OM904LA | 4.25 | 122 | Allison AT545 | 4 A |
| Solo M920 | RV | 9.2 | 6.23 | Mercedes OM904LA | 4.25 | 122 | Allison AT545 | 4 A |
| Excel L960 | RV | 9.6 | 4.23 | Cummins B | 5.9 | 160 | Allison B300R | 4 A |
| Excel L1000 | RV | 10.0 | 4.66 | Cummins B | 5.9 | 160 | Allison B300R | 4 A |
| Excel L1070 | RV | 10.7 | 5.37 | Cummins B | 5.9 | 160 | Allison B300R | 4 A |
| Excel L1150 | RV | 11.5 | 6.09 | Cummins B | 5.9 | 160 | Allison B300R | 4 A |

## SCANIA (Sweden)

| Model | Pos | | | Engine | | bhp | Gearbox | |
|---|---|---|---|---|---|---|---|---|
| L113CRL | RV | 11.7 | 5.90 | Scania DSC11 | 11.0 | 260 | ZF 4HP600 | 4 A |
| N113DRB | RV | 9.5 | 4.95 | Scania DS11 | 11.0 | 220 | Voith D863 | 3 A |
| N113DRB | RV | 10.18 | 5.64 | Scania DS11 | 11.0 | 220 | Voith D863 | 3 A |
| K93CRB | RV | 12.0 | - | Scania DSC09 | 9.0 | 283 | Scania GR801/CS | 7 M |
| K113CRB | RV | 12.0 | - | Scania DSC11 | 11.0 | 340 | Scania GR801/CS | 7 M |
| K113TRB | RV | 12.0 | - | Scania DSC11 | 11.0 | 362 | Scania GR801/CS | 7 M |
| K124IB | RV | 12.0 | 6.0 | Scania DSC12-02 | 12.0 | 360 | Scania GR801/CS | 7 M |
| L94 Axcess Floline | RV | 11.8 | 6.0 | Scania DSC9-11 | 9.0 | 220 | ZF 4HP500 | 4 A |
| L94IB | RV | 12.0 | 5.82 | Scania DSC9-15 | 9.0 | 310 | Scania GR801/CS | 7 M |
| L94IB | RV | 12.0 | 5.82 | Scania DSC9-15 | 9.0 | 310 | ZF 5HP600 | 5 A |

## VAN HOOL integral (Belgium)

| Model | Pos | | | Engine | | bhp | Gearbox | |
|---|---|---|---|---|---|---|---|---|
| T815 | RV | 12.0 | 6.00 | MAN D2866 | 11.9 | 311 | ZF S6-90 | 6 M |
| T815 | RV | 12.0 | 6.00 | Cummins L10 | 10.0 | 290 | ZF S6-90 | 6 M |
| EOS 80 | RV | 9.5 | 4.49 | Mercedes OM411LA | 10.9 | 290 | ZF S6-85 | 6 M |
| EOS 90 | RV | 12.0 | 5.95 | MAN D2866 | 11.9 | 311 | ZF 6S-1600 | 6 M |
| EOS90 | RV | 12.0 | 5.95 | MAN D2866 | 11.9 | 311 | ZF 5HP590 | 5 A |
| EOS230 | RV | 12.0 | 5.8 | MAN D2866 | 11.9 | 400 | ZF 6S-1600 | 6 M |

## VOLVO (Sweden/UK)

| Model | Pos | | | Engine | | bhp | Gearbox | |
|---|---|---|---|---|---|---|---|---|
| Olympian | RV | 9.6 | 4.95 | Volvo D10A | 9.6 | 245 | ZF 4HP500 | 4 A |
| Olympian | RV | 10.3 | 5.64 | Volvo D10A | 9.6 | 245 | ZF 4HP500 | 4 A |

Gearbox options - ZF 5HP500, Voith D863

| Model | Pos | | | Engine | | bhp | Gearbox | |
|---|---|---|---|---|---|---|---|---|
| B6LE | RV | 10.6 | 5.32 | Volvo D6A | 5.48 | 180 | ZF 4HP500 | 4 A |

Engine option - 210bhp rating

| Model | Pos | | | Engine | | bhp | Gearbox | |
|---|---|---|---|---|---|---|---|---|
| B7R | RV | 12.0 | 6.30 | Volvo D7B | 6.7 | 260 | ZF S6-85 | 6 M |

Gearbox option - ZF 4HP500

| Model | Pos | | | Engine | | bhp | Gearbox | |
|---|---|---|---|---|---|---|---|---|
| B10B | RH | 11.5 | 5.80 | Volvo DH10A | 9.6 | 245 | ZF 4HP 500 | 4 A |
| B10BLE | RH | 12 | - | Volvo DH10A | 9.6 | 245 | ZF 5HP500 | 5 A |
| B10L | RH | 12.0 | - | Volvo DH10A | 9.6 | 245 | ZF 5HP500 | 5 A |
| B10L | RH | 12.0 | - | Volvo GH10A CNG | 9.6 | 245 | ZF 5HP500 | 5 A |
| B10M Citybus | UH | 10.0 | 5.50 | Volvo DH10A | 9.6 | 245 | ZF 4HP500 | 4 A |
| B9M | UH | 10.0 | 4.80 | Volvo DH10A | 9.6 | 245 | ZF S6-85 | 5 M |
| B10M GL | UH | 12.0 | 6.20 | Volvo DH10A | 9.6 | 285 | ZF S6-85 | 6 M |
| B10M GLE | UH | 12.0 | 6.20 | Volvo DH10A | 9.6 | 360 | Volvo G8 EGS | 8 M |
| B10M SE | UH | 12.0 | 4.80 | Volvo DH10A | 9.6 | 285 | ZF 5HP590 | 5 A |
| B10MT | UH | 12.0 | 5.20 | Volvo DH10A | 9.6 | 360 | Volvo G8 EGS | 8 M |
| B12T | RV | 12.0 | 6.10 | Volvo D12A | 12.1 | 420 | Volvo G8 EGS | 8 M |

Engine options - 340 and 380bhp ratings

Codes:  sd - single decker; dd - double decker
Engine position - F Front, U Underfloor, R Rear, H Horizontal, V Vertical
Gearbox - number indicates forward speeds, A Automatic, M Manual

23

# New models galore at '97 show

AS THE MOVE towards accessible public transport gains momentum, so the Coach & Bus series of shows marks the way forward. At Coach & Bus 95, low-floor single-deckers were all the rage and since then sales have taken off. At Coach & Bus 97 it was low-floor double-deckers which stole the show. These are described on page 32 and their widespread adoption is clearly going to be slower than that of single-deckers - not least because the bus market leaders, Dennis and Volvo, are still some way away from series production.

But low-floor double-deckers created a frisson of excitement at Britain's biggest bus and coach event. Indeed they overshadowed developments in low-floor single-deckers.

The Northern Counties Paladin low-floor, unveiled quietly at Coach & Bus 95, has been slow in reaching production. During 1997 production was transferred from the Northern Counties factory at Wigan to the parent Plaxton operation in Scarborough, with the body becoming the Plaxton Prestige in the process. (With Plaxton presumably hoping that few operators would remember the Prestige name had last been used - as recently as 1991 - for an abortive 3.7m-high left-hand-drive Excalibur variant on the Volvo B12 for France.)

There were two Prestiges at the show - a Plaxton demonstrator and the first of an order for 19 for Speedlink, to be used on a temporary shuttle service connecting at Heathrow Junction with non-stop trains from Paddington on the new Heathrow Express. This was scheduled to start before the end of the year, but didn't. The dual-door Speedlink Prestige had just 30 seats, with large luggage racks occupying much of the offside front section of the saloon.

A new model which could easily have passed unnoticed was the Super Pointer Dart - SPD for short - a joint project between Plaxton and Dennis. This stretches the Pointer and Dart to 11.3m (the same length as a Leyland National) and by retaining the Dart's small wheels provides what its makers claim is the best low-floor layout on the market. The SPD cuts wheelarch intrusion to a minimum which provides the maximum floor space for seating. The 41-seat SPD had 24 seats in the low front section, compared with 20 on the 12m-long 41-seat DAF/Prestige on show alongside it. The SPD features the new front and rear styling adopted for the standard low-floor Pointer body - now Pointer 2. During 1997 all Pointer 2s were for FirstBus subsidiaries

**Marshall's troubled integral Mini appeared as the revised Mini 2, in the livery of Ealing Buses which is part of the CentreWest operation. *SJB***

and one, in Provincial colours, was exhibited by Dennis.

The success of the Dart SLF has overshadowed the comparatively poor sales of Volvo's B6LE equivalent. Volvo B6LEs were on show for Travel West Midlands (on Wright's stand); Hong Kong Citybus (on Alexander's stand), and a demonstrator exhibited by Volvo. This had a 35-seat Alexander ALX200 body.

Volvo's B10BLE, announced at Coach & Bus 95, was on show on Volvo's stand with a bare chassis and a Wright-bodied 41-seater for Greater Manchester Buses North. There was also a B10BLE, for Stagecoach Busways, on Alexander's stand. Other single-deckers in operator's liveries included an Optare Excel for Cardiff and a Wright-bodied Scania L94 for Greater Glasgow.

Neoplan's N4015 is based on a Hungarian chassis. It looked fine from the outside, but couldn't match other low-floor buses with its poor interior layout. *SJB*

Not in an operator's livery was a rather unfortunate offering from Neoplan. This was the N4015, built on a Hungarian Cspel underframe, which echoed some of the worst features of the first-generation of low-floor buses shown at the NEC in 1993. It had three steps in mid saloon - and two further steps to the rear seat. Even the attractions of a Cummins/ZF driveline are not going to overcome the disadvantages of such an untidy layout.

While low-floor double-deckers were the talk of the show, there were still a couple of conventional models at the NEC. East Lancs showed its new Pyoneer on a Dennis Arrow for Capital Citybus, while Volvo had an Olympian with Northern Counties body for London Central. Both were two-door buses. It would seem fair to forecast that the Olympian - launched by Leyland at the NEC in 1980 - has made its last NEC appearance.

The main news for full-sized coach buyers was the UK launch of Van Hool's new Alizee range. As is usual with Van Hool, it's a case of evolution rather than revolution.

The main distinguishing features of the 3.5m-high T9 range over the old T8 are a new front end and a dip in the window line over the front wheel - first seen in the UK on the Jonckheere Mistral, and subsequently adopted by Berkhof (which has owned Jonckheere since 1994). Van Hool had a fine selection of new Alizees on show including a Scania L94 for The Kings Ferry, a DAF SB3000 for Fishwick, and Volvo B10Ms for Kenzies of Shepreth, Tellings-Golden Miller and Whitelaw of Hamilton. A bigger coach - and a bigger talking point - on the Van Hool stand was an Astrobel double-decker on a Volvo B12T for Britain's most famous truck operator, Eddie Stobart. It is intended for use as a team coach for Carlisle's football club.

The new T9 models overshadowed the two EOS integrals on display, including the new three-axle 230 model, in the livery of Hallmark.

Caetano unveiled a new body, the Enigma, to replace its established Algarve II. This is a 12m-long 3.5m-high coach for fitment to Volvo B10M and Dennis

Javelin chassis - or an 8.5m-long 3.2m-high midicoach on the MAN 11.220. The first will enter service in 1998.

A rather more striking MAN was shown on that manufacturer's stand, with Spanish-built Noge body. The show vehicle was left-hand-drive, but Alf Moseley Continental will be importing right-hand-drive Noge-bodied MANs in time for the 1998 season, in addition to Marcopolo-bodied Dennises.

MAN had an NL222 low-floor single-decker on its stand, bodied by East Lancs and in the livery of Nottingham City Transport.

New bodies for small coaches were shown by Plaxton and Optare, both on the Mercedes-Benz Vario chassis. In the past Plaxton has used the same basic body, the Beaver, for both buses and coaches. At Coach & Bus 97 it launched an all-new coach body, the Cheetah, to be built at Scarborough alongside the company's big coaches. (Beavers are built at the company's Small Bus Division at Anston, near Sheffield.)

The Cheetah is quite high-built, partly to provide a flat floor with no wheelarch intrusion. A plain front dome accentuates the height, and the body has what some call a fast front, which dispenses with the rather truck-like Mercedes bonnet.

Optare launched a new Autobus Classique coach body - lower-built than the Cheetah, but with a rather upright windscreen. Optare also showed the Solera, built on a Mercedes O1120L chassis. This was a 9.2m-long 35-seater, for operators looking for something bigger than the Vario, and less expensive than a short-wheelbase Dennis Javelin, MAN 11.220 or Volvo B9M. The Solera is built in Spain by Ferqui.

Where the Solera is a fairly conventional - some might even say old-fashioned - design, Iveco announced a new model in the small coach sector which was quite the opposite. The EuroMidi 80 Maxim is a 29-seater of unusual appearance. Its long sloping snout and front overhang - coupled to a metallic red paint scheme - conjured up images of lobsters. It's hard to

see the Maxim, bodied by Indcar, being a winner for Iveco, even if it does use tried and proven components from the EuroCargo truck range. Mellor unveiled the new Opus 2 25-seat body for Iveco's 59.12.

A new name in small coaches is Isuzu, with a truck-derived coach bodied by Leicester Carriage Builders and called the Marlin. It is a 23-seater selling for around £60,000; a 33-seat version is to be launched in 1998. LCB, incidentally, is owned by the Midlands Co-op.

Small buses were in the main based on the Mercedes Vario, although Optare had its new Mercedes-powered Solo and Marshall was soldiering on with its integral Midi. This was launched at Coach & Bus 95 and early examples proved to have

**The new Van Hool Alizee made its UK debut at Coach & Bus 97. It is available on DAF, Scania and Volvo chassis. This is a Volvo B10M for Whitelaw's of Hamilton.** *SJB*

questionable standards of in-service reliability. Now branded Midi 2, Marshall claim to have got rid of the bugs. A 26-seater for CentreWest was on show, alongside a Southport & District Dart SLF with Marshall's similarly-styled Capital body. Southport & District is a trading name for MTL North.

Scania used the show to launch its 4-series range with new 9-litre and 12-litre engines. The key models are the L94 and K124, both available in a range of layouts. The L94 will replace the K93 coach and the L113 bus, while the K124 will succeed the K113 coach and is available with two or three axles.

## HOW HEAVY?

Many exhibits do not carry unladen weights, but those which did include, in ascending order:

### BUSES

| | |
|---|---|
| Marshall Midi 2 integral | 6130kg |
| Dennis Dart SLF/Marshall Capital | 7050kg |
| Dennis Dart SLF/UVG UrbanStar | 7200kg |
| Dennis Dart SLF/Plaxton Pointer 2 | 7493kg |
| DAF SB220/Plaxton Prestige | 9951kg |
| Volvo B10BLE/Alexander ALX300 | 10240kg |
| Volvo B10BLE/Wright | 10560kg |
| Volvo Olympian/Northern Counties | 10820kg |
| DAF DB250LF/Optare Spectra | 11100kg |

### COACHES

| | |
|---|---|
| Bova FLC12.280 | 10840kg |
| Dennis Javelin/UVG | 11334kg |
| Volvo B7R/Plaxton | 11520kg |
| Dennis Javelin/Plaxton | 11570kg |
| Iveco EuroRider/Beulas Intalina | 11710kg |
| Dennis Javelin/Marcopolo | 11920kg |
| EOS 90 integral | 12800kg |
| Scania K113TRB/Irizar Century | 14870kg |

**The success of the full-size Irizar Century has prompted Scania to launch a MidiCentury in the UK. Scania's range does not include any suitable midi chassis, so it has turned to MAN to provide an underframe.** *SJB*

**The new Iveco EuroMidi 80 Maxim, with body by Indcar. It is a 29-seater.** *Iveco*

# Arrivaderci Cowie

ARRIVA. No, it's not a Russian car. That was A Riva. This is Arriva. It used to be Cowie, but it found a new identity in November and, no, it's not pronounced like arrival - or even a rival - with the "l" knocked out of it.

In bus industry terms Cowie - like British Bus before it (and Drawlane before that) - had been virtually invisible on the streets, except in London where there was an embryonic corporate livery with yellow stripes. The arrival of Arriva changed all that. Arriva's logo appeared on some of Cowie's London fleets within days of the new name being announced, and a corporate livery, designed by Ray Stenning of Best Impressions, was unveiled in December.

Where FirstGroup's approach to a corporate livery (see page 4) appears a little muddled, Arriva has at least gone for it wholeheartedly, like it or not. If Arriva Passenger Services (to give the bus division its full name) owns it, it will carry Arriva livery and fleetnames - except in London where red remains the rule. However Arriva isn't only ditching old liveries. It's ditching the names too. Out go North Western, Northumbria, Midland Fox and the rest, to be replaced by Arriva serving ... whatever the location may be.

The first new buses in Arriva colours - a light turquoise and a shade of biscuit - were delivered before the end of the year and included a couple of Plaxton-bodied Dennis Darts for a new park-and-ride service in Derby.

Earlier in the year there were changes among Cowie companies in the South East. First, the Green Line operations run by Maidstone & District and Kentish Bus were taken over by London Coaches in May. Then in September Londonlinks, formed in January 1995, was wound-up, with its operations being split between Kentish Bus, South London and London & Country. Londonlinks had, of course, originally been part of the London & Country operation. At the same time, Kentish Bus operations in London were put under the control of Leaside and South London. All of this led to such unusual sights as ex-Londonlinks East Lancs-bodied Citybuses being repainted red. It also spelled the end of Kentish Bus livery on Routemasters on the cross-London 19 route.

In December Arriva bought the sightseeing operations of London Coaches which involved 81 buses, most of them open-top Routemasters. The purchase did not include the North Kent Express commuter services run by London Coaches (Kent), which remained independent.

Smallish acquisitions by Cowie companies in the South East saw

**Double-deckers for Cowie were Volvo Olympians with Northern Counties Palatine bodies. Users included Northumbria and, as seen here, Maidstone & District.** *SJB*

**Yorkshire Woollen put 30 Dennis Dart SLFs into service in 1997. They have Alexander ALX200 bodies which are unusual in being double-glazed.** *David Barrow*

County Bus take over the 16-vehicle bus operation of West's of Woodford in August, and Maidstone & District acquire the bus operations of Wealden Beeline in September. West's fleet included Wright-bodied Dennis Darts and an Optare Delta. M&D Acquired five Dennis Darts from Wealden Beeline.

Two small coach businesses changed hands in the summer, one joining Cowie, the other leaving. In May Checker Travel of Pinner (14 coaches) was bought by The Shires. And in July Link Line Coaches of Harleseden, which had been under the control of London & Country, was sold to its management. Link Line ran eight coaches and had been bought by British Bus in 1992.

In Scotland there was modest expansion by Clydeside Buses.

Three associated Greenock operations were acquired in May - Ashton Coach Hire, Coastline Express and Greenock Motor Services. Then in July Clydeside bought McGill's Bus Service of Barrhead, the last survivor of the old-established pre-deregulation independents in the west of Scotland. Bridge Coaches of Erskine was purchased by Clydeside in November.

The Cowie group took 50 Scania L113s with Northern Counties Paladin bodies. Fourteen went to The Shires. *SJB*

A number of Cowie group companies took Plaxton-bodied Dennis Darts in 1997, including Stevensons which allocated them to its XL-branded route serving Burton-on-Trent. *SJB*

Arriva owns the UK DAF bus and coach importer and this is influencing new vehicle orders. An example of this was the delivery to County Bus & Coach of nine DAF SB220s with Plaxton Prestige bodies for operation on the 57-mile long Green Line service between Harlow and Heathrow Airport. *SJB*

European expansion came in September, with the acquisition of a share in Unibus of Copenhagen.

Before Arriva arrived, Cowie decided to abandon its use of on-bus video monitors broadcasting entertainment and advertising. Known as TOPPS - The Original Passenger Picture Show - it had been launched in 1994. Passengers didn't like it.

New buses for Cowie/Arriva in 1997 included Dennis Dart SLFs with Plaxton bodies, Northern Counties-bodied Volvo Olympians, and 50 Scania L113s with Northern Counties Paladin bodies - a model which was fading from the scene as low-floor buses gained in popularity. One low-floor DAF SB220 with Plaxton Prestige body was delivered to Northumbria.

Orders for 1998 delivery included more low-floor DAFs - single-deckers with bodies by Plaxton and Alexander, and double-deckers to be bodied by Alexander. The group was also buying low-floor Dennis Darts with Plaxton bodies, and Plaxton-bodied Mercedes-Benz Varios. Conventional double-deckers for 1998, bodied by Northern Counties, will be Volvo Olympians and, for London & Country, a batch of 15 DAF DB250s.

New vehicle deliveries for Arriva Passenger Services are generally handled by Hughes DAF - to be renamed Arriva Bus & Coach from 1 January 1998.

## ARRIVA BUS AND COACH COMPANIES

Clydeside Buses
  Ashton Coach Hire
  Coastline Express
  Greenock Motor Services
  McGill's
Colchester Borough Transport
County Bus & Coach Co
  Lea Valley
  Sampsons Coaches
  ThameSide
  Town Link
Crosville Wales
Derby City Transport
  Blue Bus
  City Rider
Grey-Green
Invictaway
  Kentish Bus & Coach Co
  Maidstone & District
  New Enterprise
LDT - The Shires
  Aylesbury & The Vale
  Checker Travel
  Chiltern Rover
  Gade Valley
  Hitchin & District
  Lucketts of Watford
  Luton & Dunstable
  Network Watford
  Stevenage Line
  Stuart Palmer
Leaside Buses
London & Country
  Gem Fairtax

Guildford & West Surrey Buses
Horsham Buses
Midland Fox
  Fairtax Foxhound
  Fox Cab
  Fox Cub
  Urban Fox
Midland Red North
North East Bus
  Tees & District Transport Co
  Teesside Motor Services
  United Automobile Services
  Eden Bus Services
North Western Road Car
  Arrowline
  Bee Line
  Liverline
  Star Line
  Warrington Goldlines
  Wigan Bus
Northumbria Motor Services
  Hunters
South London Transport
Southend Transport
Stevensons
  Viking
Yorkshire Bus Group
  Selby & District
  South Yorkshire Road Transport
  West Riding Automobile Co
  Yorkshire Woollen District
    Transport Co
  Yorkshire Buses
Hughes Daf

Cowie's Crosville Cymru took two Mercedes-Benz Varios in 1997. These had Plaxton Beaver 2 bodies and were finished in a yellow livery for operation on tendered services for Conwy council. *SJB*

Clydeside Buses had a fleet which was badly in need of new vehicles. In 1997 it received 35 Dennis Dart SLFs. The body order was divided between Plaxton, with 25, and Alexander, with 10. This is a Plaxton Pointer in Paisley. *SJB*

# Easy-access 'deckers coming

DENNIS WAS FIRST off the mark in the low-floor double-deck race, with the entry into service of its first Trident in Hong Kong in September. The three-axle Cummins-powered Trident had been announced in 1996.

Back in the UK, Optare announced its plans in May, and unveiled its low-floor offering at Coach & Bus 97 in October. This was a revamped Spectra - looking pretty much like the original model of that name and with a high degree of parts commonality - but based on the low-frame DB250LF chassis which had been exhibited by DAF two years earlier at the Coach & Bus 95 exhibition.

This marries the low front section of the SB220LF, as bodied for UK operation by Northern Counties, to the standard DB250 drive-train, currently the 272bhp 8.65-litre DAF RS200 engine with a choice of ZF or Voith automatic gearboxes. The low-floor Spectra is 10.74m long on a 5448mm wheelbase - an increase in overall length of around 500mm. It is 4.17m high (13ft 8in) and has a single entrance step of 320mm. It can carry up to 80 seated passengers. At its launch Optare was quoting a price of £135,000.

The vehicle at Coach & Bus 97 was one of two ordered for evaluation by Travel West Midlands, which were to enter service in Birmingham and Dundee in early 1998. It was an 80-seater and it weighed 11100kg.

The new Spectra must spell the end of the old model. No conventional Spectras were sold in 1997, and total UK sales since the model's launch have totalled around 80 - for East Yorkshire, London Buses, Reading Transport and Wilts & Dorset.

At Coach & Bus 97 the talk of the show was the Plaxton President, a design which left all other double-deckers in the shade. This had an interior which made even the Spectra look ordinary, while the exterior marked a major step forward for its builder, Northern Counties at Wigan. The two-door President was an aluminium-framed structure with a low floor, a straight, forward-ascending, staircase and 70 seats. It was built to the new legal maximum width of 2.55m.

The President was long - 10.5m - and was based on a chassis whose manufacturer, Volvo, was unusually reticent. While Plaxton was happy to talk about the body, Volvo was happy to keep silent about the chassis. What could be deduced from looking at it was that it had a vertical engine mounted at the rear nearside corner and sitting in line with the chassis - a bit like

**The style of buses to come? Plaxton's President, built at the company's Northern Counties factory in Wigan, represented a quantum leap in double-deck design. The prototype was on a Volvo chassis. It will also be built on DAF and Dennis low-floor chassis - but not on conventional chassis such as Volvo's Olympian. *Plaxton***

he Bristol VRL of 30 years ago. The engine was fairly compact, prompting speculation that it was the 7-litre unit which once powered the Ailsa.

The engine position - and the overall length of the vehicle - point to the chassis having been developed for operation in Europe, where there would be space to have an entrance in the rear overhang. Indeed its length could prove to be its downfall. Few British fleets buy long double-deckers and London in particular has an aversion to them. The Volvo was exhibited in London red and was to enter demonstration service in the capital at the start of 1998.

Plaxton will be offering the President body on other low-floor chassis.

While Volvo had a UK-specification low-floor double-decker on show at Coach & Bus 97 but were keeping quiet, their rivals at Dennis didn't have a UK-spec bus but were broadcasting that they had won an order for 100 of a new two-axle Trident model from Stagecoach.

This shares the name and the front axle layout with the three-axle export Trident - two of which were at Coach & Bus 97 with Alexander's new ALX500 body. But at the rear the UK and export Tridents are quite different. Hong Kong's Tridents use a beefy Cummins M11 engine, while the UK model will have the familiar 8.3-litre C-series which powers the Javelin, Lance and Arrow. In the Trident this is linked to a ZF or a Voith automatic gearbox.

To launch the two-axle Trident with an order for 100 was quite a coup for Dennis. It is open to question whether the company has ever received a single order for 100 double-deck buses from a British operator, although it does regularly supply large batches to companies in Hong Kong. Those for Stagecoach will have Alexander ALX400 bodies.

While the Spectra diverted the limelight from DAF to some extent, the Dutch manufacturer did announce an order for 63 low-floor DB250s for the Cowie group. These will have Alexander bodies and delivery starts in 1998. The Stagecoach Dennises are not due to take to the streets until early 1999.

Thus 1998 will see DAF leading the low-floor double-deck business in the UK, with Dennis following at the end of the year. And Volvo? Well, there are those who reckon a rethink will be needed if the Swedish manufacturer is to make much progress - which could cost them time they can ill afford.

# Volvo aims at Javelin

WHILE VOLVO sells more coaches in Britain than any other manufacturer - and by a handsome margin - its mid-engined B10M has been facing growing competition from Dennis, DAF and Scania.

The Dennis Javelin, which is lighter and more fuel efficient than any other full-size coach available in the UK - and is generally cheaper, too - has been steadily winning more customers, and Volvo's new B7R, announced in March and unveiled at Coach & Bus 97, can be seen as a direct response to the growing success of the Javelin.

That would, in truth, be to take to narrow a view, because the B7R is aimed at Volvo markets worldwide - but it's certainly the view taken by many coach operators in the UK.

The B7R is lighter and cheaper than the Volvo B10M - and, as the "R" in the chassis code suggests, it's rear-engined. The engine is Volvo's vertical D7, with power ratings of 230, 260 and 285bhp - although only the 260bhp engine will be offered in the UK. The 6.7-litre D7 is used in Volvo's lighter trucks, and is the latest incarnation of the TD70 which powered the Ailsa double-decker in the 1970s and 1980s.

For UK operation it is offered with a choice of either a ZF S6-85 manual gearbox with a Telma retarder or, with an eye to its potential as a commuter coach, a ZF 4HP500 automatic.

Initially the B7R is available only with Plaxton bodywork. This is a variant of the best-selling Premiere 320 with simplified interior trim which is being marketed as the Prima. The launch vehicle featured a conventional chassis frame which meant that luggage accommodation was restricted, but the majority of production Prima B7Rs in 1998 will have the centre section of the frame removed, with the front and rear running units integrated into the Plaxton body - rather similar to the concept seen in 1996 with the Volvo B10M-SE, which has sold in fairly small numbers.

The first Prima B7R was sold to a Gloucestershire operator, Bevan of Lydney, and will enter service in the spring of 1998. Both Volvo and Dennis will be watching closely to see who buys Prima B7Rs as the model comes on stream in 1998. Will it be Javelin buyers switching to the new model, as Volvo hopes? Or will it be B10M customers trading down, taking the B7R for operations where they believe a lighter chassis can cope, as Dennis hopes?

But whatever the final score in the UK, Volvo's international aspirations were underlined with the announcement of the first big B7R order: 150 for operation in Iran.

# Municipal deliveries

New for Yellow Buses in Bournemouth were the company's first low-floor buses - Dennis Dart SLFs with East Lancs Spryte bodies. Yellow Buses had previously bought conventional Darts. *SJB*

The last Alexander Striders were built in 1997, for Newport Transport. There were six, on Scania N113 chassis, and they brought to 30 the number of Striders in the Newport fleet. *Alexander*

Nottingham City Transport raised a few eyebrows by ordering the moribund mid-engined Citybus from Volvo in 1997. It took ten with East Lancs Pyoneer bodies. *David Barrow*

# Premyer Pyoneers new look for East Lancs

EAST LANCS unveiled a new double-deck body in the spring of 1997 and quickly hit a snag: its name. It was launched as the Premyer - keeping up the "y" tradition of Spryte and Flyte - but the name, not surprisingly, upset Plaxton. It may be spelt differently, but it certainly sounds the same.

To address the problem the trade journal Coach and Bus Week ran a reader competition to find a new name. It would have been tempting to suggest Excalybur, (built by East Lancashyre Coach Builders) but in the end the winner was Pyoneer. Coincidentally the short-lived Premyer name was used for a body launched on a chassis which also had an identity crisis when it first appeared - the Dennis Arrow which started life as the Lance.

The basic Pyoneer aluminium body structure differs little from the Cityzen, which is available exclusively on Scania chassis. However the front end is new, and the windscreen and lower front panels share parts in common with the successful Spryte.

The first Pyoneers were for Capital Citybus, which took nine two-door models for operation on a London tendered service. A repeat order for 27 was placed by Capital Citybus at the end of the year. Further orders soon followed on Volvo Olympian chassis with 22 for rapidly-expanding Harris Bus and 15 each for Metrobus of Orpington and Nottingham City Transport. Nottingham also took 10 on Volvo Citybus chassis - the first examples of Volvo's mid-engined 'decker to take to the road since six were delivered to Northampton Transport back in 1993. A Pyoneer rebody was delivered to Dunn-Line of Nottingham, on a Volvo B10M coach chassis.

For 1998 expect to see the Pyoneer being developed to fit new-generation low-floor double-deck chassis.

East Lancs' Spryte on the Dennis Dart SLF continued to sell well, although sales of the Flyte were fairly low, on what are now

considered high-frame single-deck chassis. Three went to Black Prince of Leeds on Scania L93 chassis, while Flyte rebodies were supplied to Yorkshire Traction, on K-series Scanias.

A lengthened Spryte was unveiled at Coach & Bus 97 on the low-floor MAN NL222 chassis. This was a 43-seater in the colours of Nottingham City Transport. It had 22 seats in the step-free forward section, with two steps up to the rear seating area.

**The first customer for East Lancs' new Pyoneer body was Capital Citybus, with nine on Dennis Arrow chassis. By the end of the year Pyoneers were in service with Harris Bus, Metrobus and Nottingham City Transport. *SJB***

**The Spryte body was shown at Coach & Bus 98 on an MAN chassis - the first MAN to be bodied by East Lancs. It was in Nottingham City Transport livery. *SJB***

# New accessible mini wins orders for Optare

OPTARE HAS SOMETHING of a reputation for mould-breaking vehicles. The CityPacer, the Delta and the Spectra were all buses with trend-setting styling. The CityPacer set standards of style - if not of practicality - for small buses, which some would argue have yet to be matched. The Delta still looks modern 10 years on. Leyland's Lynx, by comparison, looks old and tired. The Spectra showed that double-deckers didn't have to look boxy.

Now comes another mould-breaker from Optare: the Solo. Launched at Coach & Bus 97, the Solo is Optare's accessible small bus - new from front to back and with a name that defines its aim, so low.

The first surprise about the Solo is its engine location. The location of the wheels right up front suggests that the Solo is a front-engined model. It isn't. The engine is at the rear. This makes it easier to provide a low floor, by dispensing with the need to have a prop-shaft running from a front-mounted engine to the rear axle.

The engine is the Mercedes-Benz OM904LA, a 4.25-litre unit rated at 122bhp and familiar to bus operators in the Mercedes Vario. It drives an Albion rear axle by way of an Allison AT545 four-speed automatic gearbox. The AT545 is also familiar to most British operators, through its fitment to the Dennis Dart.

As with the bigger Excel, Optare has gone for welded steel integral construction on the Solo. And although it's a small bus, it comes with air suspension, complete with the option of a kneeling facility which allows the front suspension to be lowered, reducing the already low entry step from 250mm to 190mm.

There are two models in the Solo range, the 8.5m M850, which can seat up to 33, and the 9.2m M920 which can seat up to 37. The Solo is a full 2.5m wide - making it wider than, say, a Plaxton Pointer 2 at 2.4m. This could affect the Solo's ability to penetrate areas which can be reached by a Mercedes Vario, as could the long wheelbase, which at 6225mm on the Solo M920 is longer than that on a 10.5m Dennis Dart SLF.

**An artist's impression of the Optare Solo, demonstrating the crisp modern look the industry expects from any new Optare model. The Solo was launched at Coach & Bus 97, with production starting in 1998.** *Optare*

The 31-seat Solo displayed at Coach & Bus 97 weighed 5480kg. Its most obvious competitor, a 31-seat Mercedes-Benz Vario with Plaxton Beaver 2 body (for Trent) weighed 4955kg. Yet the long-term question is just how long will the Vario be a competitor for the Solo? The Disability Discrimination Act will be setting new standards of accessibility which will be applied progressively to all types of local buses - including minibuses. And that could spell the end of the road for the Vario (and for the low-volume Iveco 59.12).

It could also spell the end for many of the services they run too, if the need to buy more expensive vehicles tips the balance from profit to loss - which is something the legislators seem to have lost sight of.

So while the Vario will clearly outsell the Solo in 1998 - on price rather than on specification - in the longer term the story may turn out rather differently. Remember the tale of the hare and the tortoise?

The first orders for Solos were announced at Coach & Bus 97. Wilts & Dorset, a big user of Optare MetroRiders, is taking 85, and Travel West Midlands, which bought Mercedes Varios in 1997, is to take 30. With Optare saying that Solo orders were valued at "more than £9 million" the price would appear to be approaching

£80,000 - which is getting into the Dart SLF arena. By the end of the year Optare was claiming orders for over 200 Solos, including 10 for Nottingham, eight for the Go-Ahead Group and 12 for FirstGroup.

The Optare MetroRider continues in production.

**OPTARE**

**New Coaches Too**

Optare launched a restyled Autobus Nouvelle 2 coach body on the Mercedes-Benz Vario chassis at Coach & Bus 97. The first was for Dickinson of Boston. Autobus of Rotherham was bought by Optare in 1996.

Optare is also marketing the £89,875 Spanish-built Ferqui Solera in the UK, a 9.2m-long 35-seat coach body mounted on a front-engined Mercedes O.1120L chassis. It, too, was launched at Coach & Bus 97.

Optare's Excel has in the main been bought by small operators rather than by the big groups. Timeline took nine, making it Optare's third-biggest Excel customer, after Cardiff and Reading. *David Barrow*

The Go-Ahead group, one of the pioneers of accessible buses, bought eight Optare Excels for its Coastline fleet. One heads through Whitley Bay on its way to North Shields. *SJB*

# Who owns whom...

A quick guide to the major groups and their key subsidiary companies, associated companies and principal trading names.

**Arriva** - see page 30

**Blackpool Transport Services**
Baby Blues
Blue Buses
Handybus
Seagull Coaches

**Blazefield Holdings**
Cambridge Coach Services
Harrogate & District Travel
Keighley & District Travel
    Northern Rose
London Sovereign
Sovereign Bus & Coach Co
    Welwyn-Hatfield Line
Sovereign Buses (Harrow)
Yorkshire Coastliner

**Border Buses**
    Viscount Central

**Bournemouth Transport**
Christchurch Buses
Dorset Travel Services
Vintage Yellow Buses
Yellow Buses
Yellow Coaches

**Cawlett Group**
North Devon
    Atlantic Blue
    Red Bus
    South Western
    Tiverton & District
Pearce, Darch & Willcox
    Comfy-Lux
Southern National
Taylors Coaches
West Dorset Coaches

**Durham Travel Services**
York Pullman

**EYMS Group**
Connor & Graham
East Yorkshire Motor Services
Finglands
Hull & District
Scarborough & District Motor Services
    Primrose Valley
    Scarborough Skipper

**FirstGroup** - see page 7

**Flights Travel Group**
    Central Coachways
    Excelsior
    Flights

**Go-Ahead Group**
Brighton & Hove Bus and Coach Co
City of Oxford Motor Services
    The Oxford Bus Company

The Go-Ahead Group tried the heavy-duty DAF SB220, taking six with Plaxton Prestige bodies for its Go-Ahead Gateshead company during 1997. The low floor Prestige was originally developed by Northern Counties. *SJB*

    The Wycombe Bus Company
Gateshead & District Omnibus Co
    Go-Ahead Gateshead
Langley Park Motor Co
    Gypsy Queen
London Central Bus Co
    Camberwell Clipper
London General Transport Services
    Red Arrow
    Streetline
Low Fell Coaches
Northern General Transport Co
Northern National Omnibus Co
OK Motor Services
Sunderland & District Omnibus Co
    Wear Buses
Tynemouth & District Omnibus Co
    Coastline
Tyneside Omnibus Co
    VFM Buses
Visitauto
    Metro Buses
Voyager
Victory Railways*
    Thames Trains

**Harris Bus**
Ilford Link
Lewisham Link

**London United Busways**
Airbus
Stanwell Buses
    Westlink

**Lynton Travel Group**
Airport Coaches
Biss Brothers Travel

**Metroline Holdings**
Brents Travel
Metroline Travel

**MK Metro**
Premier Buses

**Moseley Group**
Bowens
Yorks

**MTL Trust Holdings**
Coach 2000
Liverbus
Merseyside Transport
    Lancashire Travel
    Merseybus
    MTL Travel
    Sightseers
    Southport & District
    Wirral Peninsula
MTL Heysham
MTL London Northern Bus Co
    Camden Link
    MTL London
    Red Express
MTL North
Merseyrail Electrics
Regional Railways North East

**National Express Group**
Eurolines
Flightlink
Highland Country Buses
National Express
    Rapide
National Expressliners
Scottish Citylink

Gaelicbus
Skyeways *
West Coast Motor Services *
Speedlink Airport Services
Flightline
Jetlink
Taybus Holdings
Dundee Bus Co (not trading)
Tayside Public Transport Co
Tayside Greyhound
Travel Dundee
Wishart (Friockheim)
West Midlands Travel Group
Merry Hill Minibuses
Smiths Coaches (Shennington)
Travel West Midlands
West Midlands Travel
WM Buses
Your Bus
Central Trains
Gatwick Express
London & Continental Railways (17 per
cent)
Midland Main Line
North London Railways
Scotrail

**Northern Ireland Transport Holding**
Company
Citybus
Flexibus
Ulsterbus
BusyBus
Goldliner

**Nottingham City Transport**
South Notts

**Parks of Hamilton**
Trathens Travel Services

Q Drive
Eurobus
Limebourne Coaches
The Glider
Scan Coach
AVE Berkhof

**Rapson group**
Highland Scottish Omnibuses
Rapson Coaches

**Reading Transport**
Goldline Travel
London Line
Newbury Buses
Reading Buses

**Rossendale Transport**
Ellen Smith Coaches

**Southern Vectis**
Musterphantom
Solent Blue Line
Southern Vectis Omnibus Co

**Stagecoach** - see page 19

**Thamesdown Transport**
Dartline
Green Bus
Kingston Coaches

**Warrington Borough Transport**
Coach Lines
Midi Lines

**Wellglade**
Barton Buses
Rainbow

Trent Buses
Wilts & Dorset
Hants & Dorset Motor Services
Damory Coaches
Tourist Coaches
Wilts & Dorset Bus Co

**Yorkshire Traction Group**
Andrews-Sheffield Omnibus
Barnsley & District Traction Co
Lincolnshire Road Car Co
Meffan (Kirriemuir)
Strathtay Scottish
Yorkshire Terrier
Kingsman
Yorkshire Traction Co
Coachlink
Fastlink
Townlink

**Henlys plc**
Kirkby Coach & Bus
Northern Counties
Plaxton Coach & Bus
Prevost (Canada) (49 per cent)
Roadlease
National Expressliners

**Optare**
Autobus Classique

**Volvo Bus**
Drogmoller
Prevost (Canada) (51 per cent)
Steyr
Yeates Bus & Coach

* minority shareholding

# Ups and downs at UVG

AT THE START of the year UVG - formerly WS Coachbuilders and before that Wadham Stringer - seemed to be facing a reasonably bright future. It had previewed a new-look for its UniStar coach at Expocoach 96, and announced its revamped model as the S320, in March. It had concluded a deal to complete Mercedes-Benz O405N buses for Travel West Midlands. And it was selling its UrbanStar low-floor midi body in small numbers.

Then in December there was a sharp shock. The company's Waterlooville operation went into administrative receivership. Employees were laid off, and the administrators kept the business ticking over as they searched for a buyer.

Wadham Stringer came to prominence in the bus market at the end of the 1970s with its Vanguard body. Popular with local authorities for school and welfare work, it was also bought by a few bus operators - notably Darlington Transport (on Ward Dalesman chassis), Eastern National (on Bedford YMQ-S), and a few independents including A1 of Ardrossan and Metrobus of Orpington.

The Ministry of Defence became a major user of the Vanguard, and was Wadham Stringer's biggest bus customer for much of the late 1980s and early 1990s. In 1993 the company was bought by the Universal Vehicle Group, based in West Yorkshire, and renamed WS Coachbuilders. It

would be renamed again, as UVG, in 1995.

Wadham Stringer had launched a body for the Dart - the Portsdown - in 1990 but this found few buyers. In 1993 it tried fitting a coach body to the Dart - the Winchester - but this was even less successful. The Winchester body was made available on MAN's midi chassis in 1994, but with no greater success. Iveco turned to WS Coachbuilders to build bus bodies on six stock TurboCity chassis in 1993-94 - and it would perhaps be uncharitable to suggest this was because none of the mainstream bodybuilders wanted to get involved.

For the low-floor Dart SLF WS Coachbuilders called in the services of John Worker Design to carry out the styling, and the result

was the UrbanStar, launched at Coach & Bus 95 with a bus for Provincial. It didn't win many big orders, but buyers included Southern Vectis, Solent Blue Line, Kelvin Central (buying stock buses to use in a bus war), Silverwing at Heathrow for airside work, and Jones (Shamrock) of Pontypridd. The UrbanStar was also offered on the Volvo B6LE and MAN 11.190, but none were built on these chassis.

The UniStar coach, also unveiled in 1995, was in effect a civilian version of the Vanguard III bodies being built for the MoD, and was offered exclusively on Dennis Javelin chassis. The interior was perfectly acceptable, but the exterior belied the coach's rather humble origins with relatively shallow windscreens and a plain front panel. Buyers included a few well-known fleets, notably Mayne of Manchester and Go-Whittle of Kidderminster, as well as a number of smaller companies. The UniStar was available not just as a 12m coach, but in shorter variants too, right down to 8.5m.

The rather plain appearance of the UniStar was addressed in March 1997 with the announcement of the S320 which had a restyled front end bearing more than a passing resemblance to Plaxton's Premiere 320. Now UVG had a good-looking coach and at a low price - starting at £105,000 on a Dennis Javelin chassis.

This secured a few orders - but, as other manufacturers have found before - establishing any new model requires not just an acceptable product, but some measure of credibility. Buy a Dennis/Plaxton and you would pay more - but it

would also have a reasonable resale value in two years when the time came to replace it. The same couldn't be guaranteed with a Dennis/UVG.

So while operators might have welcomed the S320 in principle - in practice they weren't quite so enthusiastic.

The other new venture for UVG in 1997 was carrying out the trimming of Mercedes-Benz O405N integrals for Travel West Midlands. TWM had ordered 100, and these were being built in Germany, and then shipped to UVG for final trimming. Labour costs in Waterlooville were lower than in Mannheim. This project had only just got under way when the receivers were called in to UVG's Waterlooville plant.

The first UVG-trimmed O405N was exhibited by Mercedes at Coach & Bus 97. At the same event UVG had on display a Solent Blue Line Dennis Dart SLF with a 44-seat UrbanStar body (actually operated by Marchwood Motorways on Solent Blue Line's behalf) and an S320 coach for Chalkwell Coaches of Sittingbourne.

UVG was also building minibuses - the CityStar. Production of this model was transferred to the group's Bedwas factory in South Wales at the end of 1997.

The fate of the Waterlooville site will be sealed in the early part of 1998 with just two options: a new owner or closure.

# Mercedes attacks UK coach market ...again

IF YOU have a long memory you'll be familiar with the story: Mercedes-Benz attacks UK coach market. If that's the headline, the follow-up is: and then gives up.

Mercedes tried selling complete O.302 integrals in the UK in the 1960s. Progress was slow and it teamed up with Plaxton in 1968. Then it vanished. It reappeared in the late 1970s, with Wahl of London importing complete coaches. A few Mercedes with Jonckheere bodies found their way to Britain in the early 1980s. Then came another link up with Plaxton in 1990, which saw 25 Paramount 3500-bodied O303s being sold.

Now Mercedes is back. With the Vita.

The Vita uses an O404 underframe powered by a rear-mounted 340bhp V6 OM441 engine. It has a six-speed Mercedes gearbox, independent front suspension and disc brakes all round.

The body is built in Spain by Hispano Carroceria and actually looks not unlike the more expensive O404 integral - which Mercedes is not selling in Britain. The Vita is quoted as costing £175,000 - which is a bit more expensive than the market-leading Volvo B10M/Plaxton combination. There are two trim standards - the 53-seat Luxus and the 49-seat Gran Turismo. The latter comes with toilet and driver's bunk. Both have tinted double-glazing, an offside continental exit door and heated rear-view mirrors.

The Vita arrives at a time when British coach buyers are spoiled for choice. Volvo, Dennis, DAF and Scania are the key chassis suppliers, with MAN and Neoplan selling small numbers. Plaxton has a clear lead in bodies, followed by Van Hool and Jonckheere. But there are also Ikarus, Caetano, Irizar, Berkhof, Beulas and Marcopolo. Add to that Noge, new for 1998, and integrals from Setra, and you can see that the market has plenty of suppliers.

Will Mercedes stick it out this time round? Time will tell.

The long-standing on-off relationship between Mercedes-Benz and the British bus and coach market in fact relates only to full-size vehicles. Look at small buses and you see a very different picture.

The interest in small buses which was triggered by deregulation back in 1986 quickly saw Mercedes establish itself as the market leader in this sector.

The Mercedes has effectively been the standard IJK small bus in the 1990s and it is currently being bought by Cowie/Arriva, FirstGroup and Stagecoach - even if the numbers have dropped as the years have gone by.

**The new Mercedes-Benz O404 Vita has bodywork built in Spain by Hispano Carroceria.** *SJB*

# Dart deliveries

THE DENNIS DART is Britain's best-selling bus, and on current performance the 6,000th should enter service during 1998. That means that it's catching up on models like the Leyland National.

In 1997 most new Darts were SLF – Super Low Floor – models and they were delivered to fleets big and small throughout Britain and abroad.

The biggest Dart order from a small operator in 1997 came from Armchair Passenger Transport, which took 25 for new London tendered services. They had Plaxton Pointer bodies. The entire fleet is seen at Armchair's depot before entering service. *SJB*

The UVG UrbanStar found its way into a few fleets in 1997, from Mackie of Alloa in the north to Solent Blue Line in the south. Solent Blue Line took 14 on Dennis Dart SLF chassis for services in Southampton. *UVG*

## DART BUYERS IN 1997

Armchair, London
Bluebird, Manchester
CentreWest
Cowie Group
    Clydeside Buses
    Derby City Transport
    Grey-Green
    Guildford & West Surrey
    Maidstone & District
    Midland Red North
    The Shires
    Stevensons
    Yorkshire Woollen
CMT, Liverpool
Express Travel, Liverpool
FirstGroup
    Eastern Counties
    GCT
    Greater Manchester
    Kelvin
    Lowland Omnibuses
    Midland Bluebird
    Provincial
    Western National
Fishwick, Leyland
Ipswich Buses
Isle of Man Transport
K-Line, Huddersfield
Leon, Finningley
Lincolnshire Road Car
London Central
Mackie, Alloa
Merseypride
Metroline Travel
MTL North
Pioneer, Rochdale
Rhondda
Rossendale Transport
Shamrock, Pontypridd
Silver Star, Caernarfon
Solent Blueline
Stagecoach
    Cambus
    East London
Town & Around, Folkestone
Trent
Truronian
Universal Buses, Rochdale
York Pullman
Export
Action Bus, Canberra
Brisbane Bus Lines
Paramount Garages, Malta

Maidstone & District put Dennis Darts into service early in the year. These included the 500th low-floor SLF. They had Plaxton bodies and a stylish new fleet name which harked back to the traditional style used before the creation of the National Bus Company and its corporate identity. Ironically the new name will be short-lived, swept away by Arriva's new look. *SJB*

The last new bus for Rhondda before it was taken over by Stagecoach was a solitary Dennis Dart SLF with Wright Crusader body. Rhondda was one of the few small fleets to run Darts with Wright's original Handybus body. *Wright*

Truronian of Truro bought four Dennis Dart SLFs with Plaxton Pointer bodies. They were bought for the 50 mile route linking Perranporth with Lizard, the southernmost point on the British mainland. *SJB*

# DENNIS

Most Stagecoach Darts have Alexander bodies, but Cambus has four with Plaxton Pointer bodywork. They were bought for a cross-city service. *SJB*

In April Blue Triangle of Bootle adopted a new name and image, becoming Merseypride. A new delivery was this Dennis Dart SLF with Marshall Capital body. *David Barrow*

Express Travel took over a tendered service on Merseyside and bought eight new Dennis Dart SLFs with East Lancs Spryte bodies. Hitherto the company had been best known as a supplier of coaches to National Express. *Dennis*

The Dennis Dart SLF was bought by fleets large and small in 1997. CMT Buses of Liverpool took 12 with Wright Crusader bodies, at a cost of over £1million. Wright is a major supplier of bodies to Liverpool fleets - with MTL buying Wright-bodied Volvos and Scanias. An MTL Volvo is seen in the background. *Wright*

The idea of Dennises running in Leyland would have been unthinkable 10 years ago. Fishwick of Leyland took four Wright-bodied Dart SLFs. In 1997 Fishwick marked 90 years of operation. *SJB*

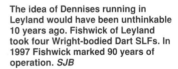

Export markets for the Dart have in the main been in the Far East and Australasia. Nearer home, operators in Malta took four - two each with bodies by East Lancs (as seen here on a wintry day in Guildford) and Plaxton. The Maltese Darts have 215bhp engines and Eaton six-speed manual gearboxes. The East Lancs Spryte bodies are 10.6m long - 0.2m shorter than usual. *SJB*

# More new models from Alexander

In 1996 ALEXANDER unveiled its new ALX200 body for the Dennis Dart SLF and Volvo B6LE, with the promise that this was the start of a new family of bus bodies covering everything from a mini to a three-axle double-decker.

Three more members of the family were launched during 1997.

First came the ALX100 on the Mercedes-Benz Vario. There is perhaps a limit to what you can do with a bus whose frontal features are defined by the chassis manufacturer's bonnet assembly. The ALX100 certainly looked better than the AM Sprint which it replaced, but it retained the unusual cross-section of the old model, with the body looking noticeably wider at the bottom than it did at the top.

The ALX100 has an aluminium frame - most bodies on the Vario are steel-framed - and it uses square-cornered gasket glazing. The circular rear lights - a styling cue common to all ALX models - are recessed to reduce the risk of lens breakage, and the standard specification includes high-level repeater brake and indicator lights mounted above the rear window. The first ALX100s were 11 divided between Cowie subsidiaries Midland Fox and Stevensons in the summer.

The next additions to the range were on show at Coach & Bus 97, the ALX300 and ALX500.

The ALX300, exhibited on a Volvo B10BLE for Stagecoach's Busways fleet (which ordered 22), is an ALX200 writ large. It is longer, at 12m, and wider too, being built to the new 2.55m width. The extra width requires different windscreens, but it would take a sharp eye to spot the difference. For Stagecoach the ALX300 has square-cornered glazing and 44 seats. The unladen weight of a B10BLE with ALX300 body is 10240kg.

ALX300 production starts in early 1998 with the Stagecoach vehicles being followed by bodies for Arriva on DAF SB220 chassis and then 150 MANs for Stagecoach.

The ALX500 is a three-axle 12m double-decker, being built initially for Kowloon Motor Bus in Hong Kong on Dennis Trident chassis. It is an impressive looking vehicle sharing its lower deck front with the ALX300. There were two on show at Coach & Bus 97, by which time the first had actually entered KMB service - making Alexander and Dennis the first UK manufacturers to have a new-generation low-floor double-decker in service, even if it was on the other side of the world.

The ALX500s - one exhibited by Alexander, the other by Dennis - were air-conditioned, with sealed tinted glazing. The interior trim looked a shade spartan by UK (and Hong Kong) standards with a pvc-type covering on the 91 seats (all with seat-belts) in place of the usual moquette. They were from an order for 182, some of which are in the livery of KMB's Long Win subsidiary, as exhibited by Dennis.

The ALX400, on two-axle low-floor chassis, will be broadly similar in style to the ALX500. It is to appear in 1998.

The new models have spelled the end for some established Alexander bodies. The last Striders were delivered in 1997 (to Newport on Scania chassis). The Dash has been dropped, as operators of midibuses have generally switched to low-floor chassis. This leaves the PS as the last old-generation single-decker - and it is expected to be phased out as the ALX300 comes on stream - plus the double-deck R-type and the Royale. Orders for both double-deck bodies were in hand at the end of 1997 - R-types for Citybus in Hong Kong and the last of 144 Royales for FirstGroup.

There were also orders for ALX400s from Arriva on DAFs and Stagecoach on Dennises.

Alexander's ALX300 body for full-size single-deck chassis looksvery much like the existing ALX200, although it is wider at 2.55m compared with the ALX200's 2.4m width. The first ALX300 was for Stagecoach. SJB

**Key new vehicle deliveries during 1997 included:**

| Operator | Qty | Vehicle | Body |
|---|---|---|---|
| A1A Travel, Birkenhead | 2 | Optare MetroRider | |
| ABC, Formby | 2 | Optare Excel | |
| Action Bus, Canberra | 25 | Dennis Dart SLF | Wright Crusader |
| Alfa, Leyland | 5 | DAF SB3000 | Ikarus Blue Danube |
| Andrews, Whiteness | 1 | Marshall Mini | |
| Armchair, London | 25 | Dennis Dart SLF | Plaxton Pointer |
| Badgerline | 6 | Volvo Olympian | NC Palatine II |
| BCP, Gatwick | 5 | DAF SB220 | Ikarus |
| Big Foot, Leeds | 1 | Scania L113 | East Lancs Flyte |
| Black Prince, Leeds | 3 | Scania L113 | East Lancs Flyte |
| Bluebird, Manchester | 4 | Dennis Dart SLF | Wright Crusader |
| Brighton & Hove | 17 | Scania N113 | East Lancs Cityzen |
| Brisbane Bus Lines | 3 | Dennis Dart SLF | Custom Coaches |
| Bristol Airport | 2 | Scania L113 | Wright Axcess-ultralow |
| British Telecom | (a) 3 | Optare Excel | |
| Bus Eireann | 9 | Volvo B10B | Wright Endurance |
| | 1 | Volvo B10L | Wright Liberator |
| | (a) 55 | Volvo B10M | Caetano Algarve |
| Cambus | 4 | Dennis Dart SLF | Plaxton Pointer |
| Capital Citybus | 9 | Dennis Arrow | East Lancs Pyoneer |
| | 16 | Volvo Olympian | Alexander R |
| Cardiff City Transport | 15 | Optare Excel | |
| CentreWest | 41 | Dennis Dart SLF | Marshall Capital |
| | 16 | Marshall Mini | |
| Cheltenham & Gloucester | 15 | Iveco 49.10 | Mellor |
| Chester City Transport | 6 | Scania L113 | Wright Axcess-ultralow |
| Citybus, Belfast | (a) 50 | Volvo B10L | Alexander Ultra |
| Clydeside Buses | 25 | Dennis Dart SLF | Plaxton Pointer |
| | 10 | Dennis Dart SLF | Alexander ALX200 |
| CMT, Liverpool | 12 | Dennis Dart SLF | Wright Crusader |
| Coastline, North Shields | 8 | Optare Excel | |
| County Bus & Coach | 9 | DAF SB220 | Plaxton Prestige |
| Crosville | 3 | Scania L113 | Wright Axcess-ultralow |
| Crosville Cymru | 2 | Mercedes Vario | Plaxton Beaver 2 |
| Delaine, Bourne | 1 | Volvo Olympian | East Lancs |
| Derby City Transport | 2 | Dennis Dart SLF | Plaxton Pointer (b) |
| | 2 | Dennis Dart SLF | Alexander ALX200 |
| Dublin Bus | 70 | Volvo Olympian | Alexander Belfast R |
| East London | 38 | Volvo Olympian | Alexander R |
| East Yorkshire | 3 | Mercedes O405 | Optare Prisma |
| Eastern Counties | 10 | Scania L113 | Wright Axcess-ultralow |
| | (a) 18 | Dennis Dart SLF | Plaxton Pointer |
| Eastern National | 13 | Dennis Lance | NC Paladin |
| | 8 | Mercedes Vario | Plaxton Beaver 2 |
| Eve, Dunbar | 1 | Volvo B6LE | Alexander ALX200 |
| Excelsior, Bournemouth | 19 | Volvo B10M | Plaxton |
| Express Travel, Liverpool | 8 | Dennis Dart SLF | East Lancs Spryte |
| FifeFirst | 3 | Dennis Dart SLF | Plaxton Pointer |
| Fishwick, Leyland | 4 | Dennis Dart SLF | Wright Crusader |
| GCT, Glasgow | 8 | Dennis Dart SLF | East Lancs Spryte |
| | 2 | Dennis Dart | Plaxton Pointer |
| Glossopdale, Glossop | 4 | Marshall Mini | |
| Go-Ahead Gateshead | 6 | DAF SB220GS | Plaxton Prestige |
| Greater Glasgow | 50 | Volvo Olympian | Alexander Royale |
| | 10 | Volvo Olympian | NC Paladin II |
| | 20 | Volvo B6LE | Alexander ALX200 |
| Greater Manchester | 25 | Dennis Dart SLF | Plaxton Pointer |
| | 55 | Dennis Dart SLF | Plaxton Pointer 2 |
| | 9 | Volvo B10BLE | Wright Renown |
| Grey-Green, London | 17 | Dennis Dart SLF | Alexander ALX200 |
| Guildford & West Surrey | 6 | Dennis Dart SLF | Plaxton Pointer |
| Hallmark, Gatwick | 5 | DAF SB220 | Ikarus Citibus |
| Harris Bus | 22 | Volvo Olympian | East Lancs Pyoneer |
| | 8 | Optare Excel | |
| Harrogate & District | 3 | Volvo B10B | Wright Endurance |
| | 3 | Volvo B6LE | Wright Crusader |
| Ipswich Buses | 6 | Optare Excel | |
| | 3 | Dennis Dart SLF | East Lancs Spryte |
| Isle of Man Transport | 25 | Dennis Dart SLF | Marshall Capital |
| K Line, Huddersfield | 1 | Dennis Dart | Plaxton Pointer |
| Keighley & District | 5 | Volvo B10B | Wright Endurance |
| Kelvin | 13 | Volvo B10M | Plaxton Premiere |
| | 15 | Dennis Dart SLF | UVG UrbanStar |
| | 2 | Scania L94 | Irizar InterCentury |
| Kowloon Motor Bus | (z) 182 | Dennis Trident | Alexander ALX500 |
| Leeds City Link | 16 | Volvo Olympian | Alexander Royale |
| Leon, Finningley | 1 | Dennis Dart | Plaxton Pointer |
| Lincolnshire RoadCar | 4 | Dennis Dart SLF | East Lancs Spryte |
| London Central | (z) 35 | Volvo Olympian | NC Palatine I |
| | 25 | Dennis Dart SLF | Plaxton Pointer |
| London Coaches (Kent) | 5 | DAF SB3000 | Plaxton Premiere |
| Longstaff, Mirfield | 1 | Dennis Lance | Plaxton Verde |
| Lothian Region Transport | 34 | Volvo Olympian | Alexander Royale |
| | 1 | Dennis Javelin | Caetano Algarve |
| Mackie, Alloa | 4 | Dennis Dart SLF | UVG UrbanStar |
| Merseypride | 1 | Dennis Dart SLF | Marshall |
| Metrobus, Orpington | 15 | Volvo Olympian | East Lancs Pyoneer |
| Metroline Travel | 60 | Dennis Dart SLF | Plaxton Pointer |
| Midland Bluebird | 4 | Mercedes O405 | Optare Prisma |
| Midland Red North | 5 | Dennis Dart SLF | Plaxton Pointer |
| MTL North | 13 | Dennis Dart SLF | Plaxton Pointer |
| Newport Transport | 6 | Scania N113 | Alexander Strider |
| North Western | 21 | Scania L113 | NC Paladin |
| Northampton Transport | 6 | Volvo B10L CNG | Alexander Ultra |
| Northumbria | 11 | Volvo Olympian | NC Palatine II |
| Nottingham City Transport | 15 | Volvo Olympian | East Lancs Pyoneer |
| | 10 | Volvo Citybus | East Lancs Pyoneer |
| Oxford Bus Company | 15 | Volvo B10B | Plaxton Verde |
| Paramount Garages, Malta | 2 | Dennis Dart SLF | East Lancs Spryte |
| | 2 | Dennis Dart SLF | Plaxton Pointer |
| Pemico, London | 10 | Dennis Javelin GX | Plaxton Excalibur |
| Pink Elephant, Stansted | 6 | Dennis Dart SLF | East Lancs Spryte |
| Pioneer, Rochdale | 2 | Dennis Dart SLF | Marshall Capital |
| PMT | 27 | Mercedes Vario | Plaxton Beaver 2 |
| | 6 | Optare MetroRider 4 | |
| Provincial | 16 | Dennis Dart SLF | Plaxton Pointer 2 |
| Reading Transport | 15 | Optare Excel | |
| Reliance, Sutton on Forest | 1 | DAF SB220 | Optare Delta |
| Rhondda Buses | 1 | Dennis Dart SLF | Wright Crusader |
| Rossendale Transport | 3 | Dennis Dart SLF | East Lancs Spryte |
| | 2 | Optare MetroRider | |
| Selkent | (z) 29 | Volvo Olympian | NC Palatine I |
| Serverse Travel | 1 | Dennis Lance | NC Paladin |
| Shamrock, Pontypridd | 2 | Dennis Lance | NC Paladin |
| The Shires | 16 | Dennis Dart SLF | Plaxton Pointer |
| | 14 | Scania L113 | NC Paladin |
| | 14 | Mercedes Vario | Plaxton Beaver 2 |
| Silver Star, Caernarfon | 1 | Dennis Dart SLF | Plaxton Pointer |
| Silverwing, Heathrow | 6 | Dennis Dart SLF | UVG UrbanStar |
| SMT | 13 | Dennis Dart SLF | Plaxton Pointer |
| Solent Blueline | 14 | Dennis Dart SLF | UVG UrbanStar |
| Sovereign | 1 | Volvo B6LE | Wright Crusader |
| Speedlink | 26 | Volvo B6LE | Wright Crusader |
| | 19 | DAF SB220 | Plaxton Prestige |
| | 5 | DAF SB3000 | Plaxton Premiere |
| Springfield, Wigan | 3 | Optare Excel | |
| Stagecoach Manchester | 5 | Volvo B10BLE | NC Paladin |
| | 35 | Mercedes Vario | Plaxton Beaver 2 |
| Stevensons | 7 | Dennis Dart SLF | Plaxton Pointer |
| Stones, Leigh | 4 | Mercedes Vario | Plaxton Beaver 2 |
| Supreme Travel, Malta | 1 | Optare Excel | |
| Swanbrook, Cheltenham | 3 | Optare Excel | |
| Tees & District | 5 | Optare MetroRider | |
| Tillingbourne | 3 | Mercedes O405 | Optare Prisma |
| Timeline | 9 | Optare Excel | |
| Town & Around, Folkestone | 1 | Dennis Dart SLF | East Lancs Spryte |

| | | | |
|---|---|---|---|
| Transmac. Macau | 15 | Mercedes Vario | Plaxton Beaver 2 |
| Travel Dundee | 20 | Volvo B10L | Wright Liberator (c) |
| Travel West Midlands | 14 | Volvo B10L CNG | Alexander Ultra |
| | 10 | Mercedes Vario | Plaxton Beaver 2 |
| (a) | 100 | Volvo B10L | Wright Liberator |
| Trent | 20 | Dennis Dart SLF | Plaxton Pointer |
| | 11 | Mercedes Vario | Plaxton Beaver 2 |
| | 5 | Volvo B10M | Plaxton Premier |
| | 3 | Optare Excel | |
| Truronian, Truro | 4 | Dennis Dart SLF | Plaxton Pointer |
| United Auto | 35 | Optare MetroRider | |
| Universal Buses, Rochdale | 3 | Optare Excel | |
| | 2 | Dennis Dart SLF | UVG UrbanStar |
| Wallace Arnold | 36 | Volvo B10M | Plaxton Premiere |
| | 15 | Volvo B10M | Van Hool Alizee |
| Western National | 6 | Dennis Dart SLF | Plaxton Pointer |
| Westlink, London | 7 | Optare Excel | |
| Williamson, Knockin Heath | 2 | Optare Excel | |
| York Pullman | 6 | Dennis Dart SLF | Plaxton Pointer |
| Yorkshire Coastliner | 4 | Volvo Olympian | Alexander Royale |
| Yorkshire Woollen | 30 | Dennis Dart SLF | Alexander ALX200 |

(a) delivered in 1996-97
(b) diverted from North East Bus
(c) diverted from Travel West Midlands
(z) delivered in 1997-98

New Volvo B6LEs were relatively rare in 1997. Harrogate & District took three with Wright Crusader bodies. *Wright*

# Forward orders

Orders announced in 1997 for delivery in 1998

| | | | |
|---|---|---|---|
| A Bus, Bristol | 1 | DAF DB250LF | Optare Spectra |
| Armchair, London | 6 | Volvo Olympian | NC Palatine II |
| Arriva (Leaside) | 63 | DAF DB250LF | Alexander ALX400 |
| Arriva (London & Country) | 13 | DAF DB250 | NC Palatine II |
| Arriva group | 51 | DAF SB220LF | Alexander ALX300 |
| Blue Bus, Horwich | 3 | Dennis Dart SLF | Plaxton Pointer |
| Bullock, Cheadle | 2 | DAF DB250LF | Optare Spectra |
| Bus Eireann | 25 | Scania L94 | Irizar InterCentury |
| Capital Citybus | 27 | Dennis Arrow | East Lancs Pyoneer |
| | 13 | Dennis Dart SLF | East Lancs Spryte |
| Delaine, Bourne | 1 | Volvo Olympian | East Lancs |
| Eastbourne | 12 | DAF DB250LF | Optare Spectra |
| EYMS Group | 15 | Optare Excel | |
| | 9 | Mercedes Vario | Plaxton Beaver 2 |
| Go-Ahead Group | 8 | Optare Solo | |
| Guide Friday, Paris | 6 | Volvo B10M | E Lancs open-top dd |
| Hong Kong Citybus | 120 | Dennis Trident | Duple Metsec |
| Kowloon Motor Bus | 50 | Dennis Trident | Alexander ALX500 |
| London Traveller | 1 | Dennis Arrow | East Lancs Pyoneer |
| Mainline | 16 | Mercedes Vario | Plaxton Beaver 2 |
| MTL London | 18 | Dennis Dart SLF | Marshall |
| Nottingham City Transport | 10 | Optare Solo | |
| RoadCar, Lincoln | 2 | Volvo Olympian | East Lancs Pyoneer |
| | 8 | Dennis Dart SLF | East Lancs Spryte |
| Shearings | 20 | Volvo B10M | Van Hool T9 |
| | 19 | Volvo B10M | Plaxton Excalibur |
| | 15 | Volvo B10M | Jonckheere Mistral |
| SMT | 21 | Volvo Olympian | Alexander Royale |
| Strathclyde PTE | 3 | Omni/Smiths electric | |
| Strathtay Scottish | 8 | Volvo Olympian | East Lancs Pyoneer |
| Travel West Midlands | 100 | Mercedes O405N | Mercedes/UVG |
| | 60 | Volvo B6LE | Wright Crusader |
| | 20 | DAF DB250LF | Optare Spectra |
| | 30 | Optare Solo | |
| Wallace Arnold | 51 | Volvo B10M | Plaxton |
| Wilts & Dorset | 85 | Optare Solo (d) | |
| | 3 | DAF DB250LF | Optare Spectra |
| Yorkshire Terrier | 4 | Dennis Dart SLF | East Lancs Spryte |
| Yorkshire Traction | 8 | Volvo B6LE | East Lancs Spryte |

(d) for delivery 1998-2000